Actes du XIVème Congrès UISPP, Université de Liège, Belgique, 2-8 septembre 2001

Acts of the XIVth UISPP Congress, University of Liège, Belgium, 2-8 September 2001

ULg
UNIVERSITÉ de Liège

I0091992

Colloque / Symposium 6.6

The Role of American Archeologists in the Study of the European Upper Paleolithic

Edited by

Lawrence G. Straus

BAR International Series 1048
2002

Published in 2016 by
BAR Publishing, Oxford

BAR International Series 1048

Acts of the XIVth UISPP Congress, University of Liège, Belgium, 2-8 September 2001
Colloque / Symposium 6.6

The Role of American Archeologists in the Study of the European Upper Paleolithic

ISBN 978 1 84171 429 5

© The editor and contributors severally and the Publisher 2002

Typesetting and layout: Darko Jerko

BAR Publishing is the trading name of British Archaeological Reports (Oxford) Ltd.
British Archaeological Reports was first incorporated in 1974 to publish the BAR
Series, International and British. In 1992 Hadrian Books Ltd became part of the BAR
group. This volume was originally published by Archaeopress in conjunction with
British Archaeological Reports (Oxford) Ltd / Hadrian Books Ltd, the Series principal
publisher, in 2002. This present volume is published by BAR Publishing, 2016.

Printed in England

BAR
PUBLISHING

BAR titles are available from:

BAR Publishing
122 Banbury Rd, Oxford, OX2 7BP, UK
EMAIL   info@barpublishing.com
PHONE   +44 (0)1865 310431
FAX   +44 (0)1865 316916
www.barpublishing.com

TABLE OF CONTENTS

"AMERICAN" PERSPECTIVES ON THE EUROPEAN UPPER PALEOLITHIC? AN INTRODUCTION

Lawrence Guy STRAUS

REFLECTIONS

Some people - including ones who graciously did participate in the symposium at Liège by giving oral presentations - thought that the idea for a symposium on "the role of American archeologists in the study of the European Upper Paleolithic" was problematic. They would argue - quite justifiably - that there is no single American "take" or perspective on this subject - either now or in the past. Each individual scholar brings her or his own point of view and intellectual baggage to the study of the later Old Stone Age and to imply the existence of an American position or paradigm (in presumed contradistinction to a "European" one) is simply wrong and, in fact, might be seen as raising the (unproductive) specter of "national schools". It may surprise some to learn that I share their apprehension of just such simplification and misunderstanding. After 30 years of "doing" Paleolithic and Mesolithic prehistoric archeology in four countries of Western Europe, I am heartened by what I see overall as a **rapprochement** - not only methodological, but also theoretical - between many practitioners based in the Old World and in the New. On the other hand - as I have long expressed (e.g., Straus 1987) - I share my colleague Geof Clark's (e.g., Clark 1991) belief that there are some deep-seated ("paradigmatic") differences in how the Paleolithic record is perceived and how it is seen as being interpretable between archeologists trained within the North American anthropological tradition and prehistorians educated within the culture-historical tradition established in France and still dominated by French scholarship. The difference is clearly much less marked between North Americans and Britons (where archeology is more closely associated with anthropology, although more commonly taught in separate academic departments than is the case in the U.S. or Canada), and certainly there are many points of similarity between Anglo-Americans and Scandinavians in their culture-ecological and social approaches to the Mesolithic. One can even argue that there are large areas of commonality of interest between American and Central/ Eastern European/ Russian (ex-Soviet bloc) archeologists in stressing the reconstruction of past lifeways, site structure, subsistence etc. (in contrast to the great stress on artifact typology, archeo-culture classification and phylogenetics that have tended to dominate French Paleolithic prehistory, which in turn had enormous influence in adjacent countries such as Spain, Italy, Portugal or Belgium).

The French-dominated culture-historical approach over more than a century has clearly placed paramount stress on interpreting differences and similarities among artifact assemblages as indicative of traditions ("**civilisations**" in French) with significance (at least assumed to be) akin to ethnic groups in the modern (or at least recent) world. Pre-history is seen as literally writing the ethnohistory of the past by means of bones, sherds and/or stones. The key is the term "prehistory" - this is seen as a fundamentally **historical** enterprise (sometimes linked more closely to Quaternary geology, and at other times merely an appendage of history - as reflected in the academic departmental placements of prehistorians).

Although things are perhaps beginning to change a bit in response to the transnational academic, funding and employment facilities afforded by the European Union, it has been my observation that prehistorians often study, do research and obtain professional positions not only within their own country, but also within their native region or province. In short, they are writing "their" own pre-history (at least by extension of residence and often several generations of familial attachment to a particular place). Europe, with its long, rich (and newly renewed) traditions of regionalism, linguistic differences and even separatism (in reaction to the trend toward central state domination begun during the Renaissance), naturally sees the archeological record in terms of cultural divisions. This is, I believe, deeply engrained in the lifelong experience and education of European prehistorians.

In contrast, most American archeologists interested in the European Upper Paleolithic (leaving aside the Middle Paleolithic, since one cannot assume that Neandertals necessarily had or knew of the concept of ethnicity), are far distant in their life experiences from European realities (or regionalist myths). Perhaps one could partially except Anta Montet-White, Olga Soffer, or even myself, given our direct European roots. But, by and large, American archeologists who study European materials are not studying "their" own prehistory in any visceral sense. (Ironically, the same is true of Euro-American archeologists who study the prehistory of Native Americans - it is not **their** past and can be viewed dispassionately, as the subject matter of a natural and social science, not as history per se.[Straus n.d.]) It is not at all hard to understand why, in America, archeology is considered by most to be a social science (albeit with close practical ties the earth and material sciences, as well as to applied physics and chemistry) and is housed in departments of anthropology or in museums of natural history or science. There is simply more emotional **distance** between most American archeologists and the objects of their research than may be the case among many European prehistorians working within and attached to their own regions.

With the concern for science and the testing of ideas, American archeologists are interested in **explaining** variability by entertaining alternative hypothesis, not by simply accepting **a priori** that all or most variability is "cultural" (i.e., ethnic or social) in character. This was the basis of the Binford-Bordes debate. But this point of does not imply that American archeologists deny the existence of more or less marked ethnicity in the past (depending on such key variables as human demographic density, geographic characteristics of territories, resource types and distribution, etc.) or the potential ability of archeology to elicit at least hints thereof. In fact, one of the founding and optimistic tenets of "processual" archeology was the idea that one could get at aspects of past life beyond dating, subsistence, etc., by means of identifying and analyzing "sociotechnic" and "ideotechnic" artifacts, to use Lewis Binford's terms from his memorable, now 40-year-old article, "Archaeology as Anthropology" (1962). The problem is **how** to determine **which** attributes of the prehistoric record might be informative of ethnicity . This problem is subject to theory building and logical bridging arguments - but not to mere presumption.

And the really interesting "big" question is why, to what extent and under what circumstances did ethnicity (territorialism, emblematic stylistic marking, exclusion, etc.) arise? This is a question of immense anthropological, social science interest. And of course the question of ethnogenesis is ultimately also of historical interest. Thus there is great potential for commonality of interest between anthropological archeologists and prehistorians precisely in the fascinating attempt to get at the existence of social groups and cultural traditions in the Upper Paleolithic.

On the other hand, it is clear that developments in terms of excavation and recovery methodology and archeological and interdisciplinary analyses (sedimentology, micromorphology, palynology, paleobotany, archeozoology, lithic microwear, isotopes, etc.) have proceeded in parallel on both sites of the Atlantic, such that there is really a shared understanding of how sites should be dug and studied, with an aim toward doing as close to total collection, recording and analysis as possible. This seems to work out well (as demonstrated by the existence of several longstanding Euro-American collaborations in individual excavation projects), despite the existence of possible nuanced differences in interpretive foci. Indeed, those differences of viewpoint (e.g, González Morales 1991; Straus 1991) are ultimately healthy and interesting, fostering the kind of dialogue that is sometimes touted as necessary for "multi-vocal" interpretation of the prehisitoric record by post-processual theoreticians of archeology (see also Dibble & Debénath 1991). The cross-fertilization of ideas and expertise, especially in technical, but critically important areas such as archeozoology, has been encouragingly productive and undoubtedly stimulated by such initiatives as Arthur Spiess', Lewis Binford's and Richard Klein's studies of faunal remains. Similar has been the back-and-forth development of lithic micro-wear analysis: begun by the Russian S.A.Semenov, but then expanded by a large number of Americans, beginning with L.Keeley and continuing with others, some of whom (have) resided in Europe for long periods of time and influenced many native European workers (e.g., Anderson-Gerfaud, Moss, Dumont, Newcomer, Unger-Hamilton, Plisson, Caspar, et al.). The cross-publication of research done in Europe in outlets both there and in the U.S. has also broken down barriers, but the linguistic "imperialism" of English (and the flagrant ignorance of non-English languages by growing numbers of American students) is quickly (and in my opinion, unfortunately) replacing the earlier dominance of French as the **lingua franca** of prehistoric archeology. Bi- (or tri-) lingualism must be stressed in the education of the coming generations of researchers, if for no other reasons than practical diplomacy and to combat narrow-mindedness and ignorance of vast portions of the record!

For better or worse, Paleolithic excavation projects (with all their ever-more-numerous and technical attendant multi/ interdisciplinary analyses) require major funding, and increasingly the American model for proposal design, review and institutional funding is being emulated in Europe. The European Science Foundation may in many ways mimic the U.S. National Science Foundation in its support of archeology, and certainly European nation-states and - as in the case of Spain - even regional governments - often with EU aid - are now tending to fund individual projects on a grant-by-grant basis, even when the older "prehistory institute" model may continue to exist, as in France (CNRS) or Germany. Even American-style "cultural resource management" (preventative-cum-salvage archeology) is taking hold in Europe, down to the creation of private contracting firms (as in newly entrepreneurial Spain), but with the additional wrinkle of archeologist labor unions (as in France). In short, research is being rationalized, administratively measured, judged and managed. These fundamental facts of life in the conduct of prehistoric research are also helping to close the trans-Atlantic gap.

Nonetheless, the important theoretical ramifications of the difference between the historical perpective favored by most continental Europeans and the anthropological one characteristic of many Americans remain real and valid. These differences of viewpoint may amount to paradigmatic divisions, despite increased blurring. One should not harp too much on these differences, however. They themselves have deeply rooted historical and cultural **raisons d'être**, but are not irreconcilable. Neither point of view is necessarily all right or all wrong and the hope (my hope - as one with feet on both sides of the Atlantic) is that the accumulating effect of contact, collaboration and discussion will make for a healthier, fuller science and art of prehistoric research and understanding of our common - albeit remote - human past (Straus n.d.).

THE PAPERS

Not all the people who gave papers in the Liège UISPP symposium are represented in this volume; some

declined to provide written versions, feeling, I believe, that it was perhaps not good to "reify" the notion of differences between "national" or "continental" schools of prehistoric archeology. This is a point of view that I of course also respect. Others were simply overwhelmed with other work and I had set a fairly tight deadline. I do particularly miss the contributions of Olga Soffer and the dynamic, long-term trans-Atlantic collaborative team of Jean-Philippe Rigaud and Jan Simek. These three have shown by their work over the years just how productive international cooperative research can be and how flimsy the supposed walls of paradigmatic difference may be.

The papers that are published here represent a diversity of backgrounds, views and experiences among both European prehistorians commenting on the American role in various European countries and among Americans who have worked in Europe and who discuss various aspects of the present and past effects of this activity.

Nuno Bicho - trained both in Portugal and in the U.S. - discusses the remarkable impact that the fairly recent involvement of a few Canadian and American researchers (notably A.E.Marks) has had on the study of the Paleolithic and Mesolithic of Portugal, in terms of fieldwork, new kinds of research questions and analyses, and training.

Harvey Bricker - the most veteran of the Americans represented - describes the pioneering methodological advances promoted by his professor, Hallam Movius, at the seminal excavation of the Abri Pataud, and is perhaps a bit too pessimistic concerning the influence of that research in the optimistic "American" years not long after the end of World War II.

Geof Clark - with lengthy experience both in Spain and Jordan - reprises his longstanding views on the importance of paradigmatic differences between Americans and Europeans who study the European Upper Paleolithic. He takes what is probably the toughest line of anyone who is interested in this topic, being deeply impressed by what he sees as the lasting influence of the "French" culture-historical approach throughout Western Europe (notably Spain) and the Near East.

Frank Harrold - acknowledged on both sides of the Atlantic as an expert on the Chatelperronian of France and Spain and steeled by Epigravettian fieldwork in Albania - takes a perhaps more measured, diplomatic, and historically informed approach in his discussion of similarities and differences between American and European scholarship on the Upper Paleolithic.

Janusz Kozlowski - the dean of Upper Paleolithic researchers in Central Europe and a living encyclopedia of prehistory for the whole continent - succinctly lays his finger on the main theoretical divergences and potetntial synergy between the culture-historical and processual perspectives, having had long, fruitful contact with a very wide circle of researchers (many his collaborators) from Eastern, Central and Western Europe, America and Israel - including ample experience with Soviet-style archeology.

Marcel Otte - a powerhouse in research spanning the European continent and beyond (from Morocco to Turkey) and a leading spokesman for the historicist perspective - appreciates the varied American role and sees a balance of both good and less good as having resulted from this involvement (which no doubt includes our own personal collaboration in Belgian excavations during 5 fruitful years).

Martin Street - a Briton born, bred and trained, but employed and based for a long time in western Germany - has the unique role as a non-continental European discussing the discrete, but important role of Americans who have worked on the Paleolithic and Mesolithic of Germany, and who, to one degree or another, have become part of the establishment in that country, which is known for its technical excellence in prehistoric archeological research, but reluctant to worry very much about "theory".

I (Lawrence Straus) - with prehistoric archeological roots in Southwest France, "processualist"-oriented training at the Universities of Chicago and Michigan, a long teaching career at the University of New Mexico in the company of Lewis Binford, and a continuous trajectory of field research in Spain, France, Portugal and Belgium over the last 30 years - tries to take a balanced and historically-rooted approach to the deep-set, but fairly recent differences in interpretation of the Upper Paleolithic record on the two sides of the ocean, arguing that they mainly have to do with differing definitions of the concept of "culture", but stressing many areas of agreement, especially in terms of excavation and analytical methodologies.

Jiri Svoboda - one of the leading and most dynamic members of the "young generation" of Czech prehistorians - stresses the long, independent tradition of Upper Paleolithic research in Moravia and acknowledges the importance of the genuine and equal collaborations with American specialists that have fairly recently developed for the study of both paleontological and archeological materials, particularly from the Pavlovian culture.

Randy White - a leading expert on the personal adornment of Early Upper Paleolithic peoples and an intimate connaisseur of the environment, sites and prehistory of the classic Périgord region...and a Canadian - reminds us of the complex history of the special relationship between American (and Canadian) archeological expeditionaries and their French interlocutors and colleagues in the "heroic" age just before and after World War I. He takes the novel approach of showing how the French (notably the great Denis Peyrony) seem to have viewed the likes of McCurdy, Field, Ami, Pond and Collie as lesser evils than the "looter" and German-Swiss Otto Hauser, probably for reasons of chauvinism, despite the equally suspect nature and ultimately deleterious impact of the collecting practices of the Americans.

The papers represent a range of opinions, but generally stress the productive - if sometimes unnecessarily tense or theoretically overblown (especially in the 1970s through 1980s) - nature of the trans-Atlantic relationship. But they are short and few, and thus are far from representative of all that could be written on this epistemologically interesting subject. They should be regarded as first attempts to outline the history of collaboration in the study of the Upper Paleolithic of Europe by Americans and Europeans and to discuss some of the key issues in the "conversation" about theories and methods that has been going on now for the better part of a century, but with an "explosion" of American involvement in only the past four decades. I hope these papers do stimulate further reflection and discussion, without provoking suspicion or acrimony.

ACKNOWLEDGEMENTS

Mr. John Rissetto and Dr. Rebecca Miller assisted most importantly with the technical aspects of preparing this volume for publication in the series of Proceedings of the XIV Congress of the UISPP, held in Liège (Belgium) in September, 2001. I also thank my friends, Professors Marcel Otte and Janusz Kozlowski respectively for organizing the Congress and for allowing the symposium to be held under the auspices of the Commission on the European Upper

Paleolithic. My participation was made possible by the University of New Mexico College of Arts & Sciences and *Journal of Anthropological Research.*

Department of Anthropology
University of New Mexico
Albuquerque, NM 87131 USA
lstraus@unm.edu

BIBLIOGRAPHY

BINFORD, L. , 1962, Archaeology as anthropology. *American Antiquity* 28, p.217-225.

CLARK, G.A., 1991, A paradigm is like an onion: reflections on my biases. In *Perspectives on the Past*, edited by G.A. Clark. Philadelphia: University of Pennsylvania Press, p.79-108.

DIBBLE, H. & DEBENATH, A., 1991, Paradigmatic differences in a collaborative research project. In *Perspectives on the Past*, edited by G.A. Clark. Philadelphia: University of Pennsylvania Press, p.217- 226.

GONZALEZ MORALES, M., 1991, From hunter-gatherers to food producers in northern Spain. In *Perspectives on the Past,* edited by G.A. Clark. Philadelphia: University of Pennsylvania Press, p.204- 216.

STRAUS, L.G., 1987. Paradigm lost: a personal view of the current state of Upper Paleolithic research. *Helinium* 27, p.157-171.

_____, 1991, Paradigm found? A research agenda for study of the Upper Paleolithic and post-Paleolithic in SW Europe. In *Perspectives on the Past*, edited by G.A.Clark. Philadelphia: University of Pennsylvania Press, p.56-78.

_____, n.d. Reflections of an archeological "outsider": an American student of the European Upper Paleolithic on the peopling of the Americas. In *Prehistoria y Sociedad: Investigación Arqueológica con Impacto Social y Gestión del Patrimonio Histórico*, edited by P.Arias. Santander: Universidad de Cantabria (in press).

THE IMPACT OF AMERICAN ARCHAEOLOGY IN THE STUDY OF THE PORTUGUESE UPPER PALEOLITHIC

Nuno Ferreira BICHO

Résumé: Les études du Paléolithique au Portugal ont eu un rôle important en archéologie vers la fin du 19ème et début du 20ème siècle. Cette importance, cependant, a diminué brusquement jusqu'aux années 1980. Au milieu de cette décennie, un groupe d'archéologues américains commencèrent à travailler au Portugal et changèrent la nature de la recherche du Paléolithique portugais. Ce changement s'est produit tant au niveau universitaire, avec la formation des étudiants gradués portugais, comme dans les fouilles, avec le travail financé par des agences américaines, comme par exemple la National Science Foundation. En conséquence, l'étude du Paléolithique supérieur est devenue un des sujets les plus importants de l' archéologie au Portugal.

Abstract: Paleolithic studies in Portugal had an important role in archaeology in the late 19th and early 20th centuries. This importance, however, decreased sharply until the 1980's. In the middle of that decade, a group of American archaeologists started to work in Portugal and changed drastically the nature of archaeological research on the Portuguese Paleolithic. This change occurred at the academic level, with the training of Portuguese graduate students, as well as in the field, with work funded by American agencies, such as the National American Foundation. As a result, the study of the Upper Paleolithic has became one of the most important fields of archaeological work in Portugal today.

INTRODUCTION

As in other areas of Europe, the study of the Portuguese Paleolithic started as early as the mid-19th century. Fieldwork was carried out by geologists from the National Geological Survey (Serviços Geológicos de Portugal) created in 1848. The main geologists were Carlos Ribeiro, well-known from the "Eolith question and Tertiary man" (Grayson 1983, 1986) and Joaquim Filipe Nery Delgado. The results of their work in caves, such as Furninha & Casa da Moura in Portuguese Estremadura, indicate a fairly advanced methodology of excavation and recording for the time. Delgado (1867) systematically questioned certain data (see Zilhão 1993), showing that he was presaging the future of archaeology with Middle Range Theory and the development of the study of site formation processes.

The second stage of development of Portuguese Paleolithic archaeology took place in the early to mid-20th century, with the work of Henri Breuil. In fact, his work defined the paradigms, both methodological and theoretical for most of the future work that would take place on the Portuguese Paleolithic nearly until the end of the century. Breuil brought from France the cultural sequence that would, since then, be applied to the Paleolithic in Portugal. Thus, Portugal became marked by the application of named cultural entities such as the Acheulean, Mousterian, Aurignacian, Gravettian, Solutrean and Magdalenian. These were defined in the same manner as in France and Northern Spain, and, naturally, erased all the regional diversity that may have existed in Portugal, as well as all the ability to recognize differences between the Portuguese and the French Paleolithic. This influence remains in the study of Portuguese prehistory still today.

Breuil's work started in 1918 with his first visit to Portugal, when he identified some Paleolithic material from Casa da Moura. He returned later, during the Second World War, together with Georges Zbyszewski, a Polish geologist also escaping from the Nazi occupation of much of Europe, except Iberia. Their work, based on surveys mostly of Pleistocene terraces and raised beaches of central and southern Portugal, resulted in a detailed cultural and stratigraphic sequence for the Portuguese Paleolithic (Breuil and Zbyszewski 1942, 1945). This sequence was structured based on three aspects: a) type fossils, which in most cases had been defined originally for the French archaeology; b) the altimetry of raised marine beaches and fluviatile terraces and the geological relation among them, resulting in a time sequence; c) and the "series method", based on the physical condition of the lithic artifacts, such as chemical and physical weathering, also known as "patina" and "edge freshness". The assemblages - in almost all cases surface collections - were arranged in series, corresponding to a supposed chronological order, with the oldest artifacts being those marked by heavy weathering, strong patina and significantly rolled. This method and sequence eventually proved to be erroneous. The case of the Mirian (Raposo and Penalva 1987; Raposo 1989) is the best example thereof. The Mirian is now known to be a Holocene industry in southern Portugal. It appeared during Epipaleolithic times, but its technology kept being used during, at least, the Chalcolithic period. According to Breuil, the Mirian was initially a facies of the Acheulean, and progressively became younger, passing by the Mousterian, Upper Paleolithic and finally reaching the Epipaleolithic during Holocene times.

Paleolithic research after Breuil followed his methods and his sequence, by both Portuguese archaeologists, such as Manuel Heleno (1956), and by French researchers who worked in Portugal for short periods of time. Among these, Jean Roche was the most important, not only for his work in sites such as Lapa do Suão and Salemas (Roche 1964, 1977, 1979, 1982; Roche and Ferreira 1970), but also for influencing a few Portuguese archaeologists who are now among the professors still teaching in the Portuguese universities.

THE IMPACT OF AMERICAN ARCHAEOLOGY IN PORTUGAL

During the late 1970's and early 1980's, Portugal experienced new interest in Paleolithic archaeology. This was marked by the work of a group self-named the "Group for the Study of the Portuguese Paleolithic" - GEPP . The work of this group focused on two main areas of research: the Tagus valley around Vila Velha de Rodão, near the border with Spain, and Estremadura, mainly the Rio Maior and the Atlantic coastal areas. In practical terms, most of the research in those areas was conducted by two young scholars, Luis Raposo and João Zilhão. The first surveyed new areas around Rodão, finding some of the most important Lower and Middle Paleolithic sites in Portugal, such as Monte Famaco, Vilas Ruivas and Foz do Enxarrique. Due to the importance of these

sites, Raposo found his research interests converging on the Middle Paleolithic.

Zilhão, while starting his research also in the Rodão area, turned to the Portuguese Estremadura region and to the Upper Paleolithic, both with new sites such as Caldeirão cave, or by reviewing the old sites excavated by Heleno some 40 years earlier. Both Zilhão and Raposo, although working separate, diverged from the traditional school of Breuil's systematics. They started to use the typological systems of Bordes and Sonneville-Bordes and Hours for respectively the Middle and Upper Paleolithic. Also, parallel to papers in Portuguese, they also published some of the interesting results that they had gathered with their new excavations in international journals. Thus, the new data, as well as the new researchers, started to become known outside of Portugal.

It was in this context that during the mid-1980s that Portugal saw the arrival of three New World archaeologists with strong interests in the Portuguese Paleolithic and Mesolithic: David Lubell from the University of Alberta, Anthony Marks from Southern Methodist University, and Lawrence Straus from the University of New Mexico. Their first visits to the National Museum of Archaeology in Lisbon clearly changed the path of the Paleolithic studies in Portugal, although then it would be hard to guess such a development. From these visits, they established contact with some of the local researchers, among them Raposo and Zilhão for the Paleolithic and José Arnaud for the Mesolithic.

The initial contacts were used to start collaborative projects in Portugal. Besides the normal ethical and cordial relations between the two groups that took place and helped establishing those projects, there were also different reasons for both sides to start these programs.

Portuguese funding for archaeology, and more so in the case of Paleolithic and Mesolithic, had been scarce to non-existent. This limited funding was given by the government on a yearly basis. One could not prepare a mid- to long-term project, because funding was decided upon every year based on a simple excavation permit for a single site. Of course, this situation also reflected the type of research that took place, as well as the paradigm of Portuguese archaeology at the time (and scientific research in general – remember that only a decade after the end of nearly half a century of dictatorship had passed, during which time science had not been welcome): archaeology was carried out at a single site for as long as possible, and, if possible, the whole site would be excavated as the life work of a single archaeologist. Thus, money was very scarce for Paleolithic archaeology and was usually granted to excavate a single site; very little money was used for dating or for studies other than lithic analysis. By the end of the 1980s there were fewer than 2 dozen dates for the whole Paleolithic and Epipaleolithic of Portugal. The collaborative Luso-American projects brought about the possibility of establishing long-term research in Portugal. Also, it allowed for a change in perspectives from the single site to regional archaeology within structured projects.

On the New World side, a variety of reasons for working in Portugal seemed to be important. The first was the lack of serious research in Portugal, which, once started, could uncover important data, different from the record known from the traditional core areas of Paleolithic research: SW France and Northern Spain. Of course, this was likely related to a time when France did not make things easy for foreign researchers to work there. Also, the competition for finding new sites in France was certainly difficult. Thus, Portugal seemed a good research area, where very little work had been carried out, new sites could be found, and the local archaeologists had interest in starting international research projects. Of course, all these aspects were also marked by the fact that the law required that a Portuguese archaeologist be responsible for the work, as well as for the annual excavation reports. In any case, work started almost immediately with different projects, respectively with Marks working in the Upper Paleolithic of Rio Maior with Zilhão and with Raposo in the Lower Paleolithic of Alpiarça (Tagus valley), Straus with Zilhão looking mostly for cave sites in Estremadura and in the South (Alentejo & Algarve) with Arnaud *and the geologist, J.A. Crispim, and Lubell also in Estremadura and in the South working mostly with Arnaud. Later, this group grew with the addition of C. Reid Ferring from the University of North Texas, who worked in conjunction with Marks and Zilhão.

Another important aspect was the economic one. The Portuguese economy was going through bad times, early in the process of reaching European Common Market standards. The US dollar could work small miracles in Portugal. Thus, a five year project cost very little money and, therefore, was certainly in good shape to compete for money within the NSF funding system when compared with projects to take place in other areas of the world.

Clearly, the common denominator of all these projects was survey for important new sites with long stratigraphies and good faunal preservation. Unfortunately, no sites were found with those two characteristics, but the work that resulted from the different projects helped to clarify a serious of erroneous cultural and chronological attributions made in the past. Also, several new open-air sites were found, that made possible the construction of a new chrono-cultural sequence for Portuguese Estremadura. The number of absolute dates was vastly increased, and in fact, these projects produced most of the data used for the new regional syntheses for the Upper Paleolithic that have been published during the last 15 years.

But the impact of American archaeology in Portugal went further than the mere increase in the amount of data or in the number of new sites. In fact, these were the least important factors in this process. It can be said that the impact of American archaeology in Portugal marked Portuguese research in two other forms. The first was at the level of graduate studies. There was a strong interest and concern on the part of some of these archaeologists in the higher education of Portuguese students, as well as the use of Portuguese data for Masters and Ph.D. degrees. Thus, a few Portuguese became graduate students at the University of Alberta and at Southern Methodist University. Among them, a total of four Masters degrees and two Ph.D.'s were finished. In addition to these, a few American graduate students came to Portugal and finished their degrees with archaeological material from the Portuguese Paleolithic & Mesolithic. In fact, we have now a total of four Ph.D. dissertations that resulted from those initial efforts (Vierra 1992; Bicho 1992; Thacker 1996; Almeida 2000). It needs to be said, however, that there was also a second intention in funding these students. The Portuguese students, once in the field, took care of many, if not all, the logistical aspects of the projects. Of course, this was good for both parties, since the American archaeologists did not need to worry about the language, bureaucracy and other different aspects of the yearly project set-up, and in return, these students learned the mechanics of the system. Although it may not seem important and even a bit imperialistic in form, it certainly was one of the best aspects of the learning process while in graduate school.

This academic process, did not limit itself to American dissertations, and at least one of these U.S. scholars, Marks, was also the advisor for Zilhão and Raposo's

Ph.D. dissertations, although the latter has not finished yet. In addition to these dissertations at Portuguese universities, but done under the supervision of American professors, there is already what can be called a second generation of doctoral degrees, both in Portugal and in the US, resulting from those first Ph.Ds. In fact, these are being completed, either under their direction or as a result of their projects.

From a very simple statistical point of view, American archaeology is responsible, directly or indirectly, for all the existing dissertations on the Portuguese Paleolithic and Epipaleolithic. There were no Ph.D. dissertations on the Paleolithic in Portugal or about Portugal before the arrival of the New World archaeologists. And, all those that have been finished were either carried out in an American university or had an American professor as advisor.

The second important aspect was a change in methodological and theoretical paradigms. I referred earlier to the general situation of Paleolithic archaeology in Portugal during the 80s. I did not, however, mention the status of archaeology as a science within the general scientific organization of Portugal. In fact, archaeology, as in other European countries, was within the academic discipline of History. The academic departments with instruction in archaeology were those of History. It was only during the 1980s that the first degree in archaeology appeared, but it was still a minor, with history as the student's required major. Archaeology has only within the last couple of years become a degree field in itself, separated from History. At the same time that Portugal is now seeing a separation between the two fields, Archaeology is clearly forming a different area of study- Cultural Heritage- together with Art History and Museology.

Another important aspect of Portuguese archaeology has been the concept and definition of culture. Not surprisingly, the definition of culture was essentially historical, and strongly marked by the idea of ethnicity. It seems that the most important operational tool of Portuguese Paleolithic archaeologists was (and in certain cases still is) the idea of cultural traditions. In fact, the concept of "cultural tradition" had an ethnic meaning that allowed the archaeologist with a single word to define culturally a group of artifacts. Thus, long-term "cultural traditions", such as Mousterian or Solutrean, were self-contained, self-defined entities with stylistic attributes and supposidly functioned as "real prehistoric socio-cultural entities" (Straus 2001). They were, in practical terms, used as

taxonomic units. They were never defined, except by comparison with the homonymous French cultural traditions, and everybody knew intuitively "exactly" what they meant.

In summary, these cultural traditions worked as a taxonomic tool for defining a chrono-cultural status of the lithic assemblage. Unfortunately, there was not even the distinction made by Harrold (2001) between cultural reconstruction and cultural process, since very little of either was carried out. Paleolithic archaeology in Portugal was restricted to lithic artifact descriptions and listing. Very little or no importance was given to fauna, even when present, and no true paleoenvironmental studies were ever carried out.

With the new Luso-American projects, the paradigms clearly changed. Not only did Portuguese archaeology gain an appreciation of the importance of other archaeological data sets such as fauna or pollen, but it also started to learn that there is an anthropological perspective necessary for the reconstruction of the cultural process. This, of course, necessarily means that Portuguese Paleolithic archaeologists were ready scientifically to accept the distinction between reconstruction and cultural process. Therefore, the definitions of the long-standing cultural traditions used as taxonomic units, were essentially put aside, along with the old type fossil concept. Although new typologies were used, Paleolithic archaeologists, started to go even further. They resorted to technological studies, although following mostly the French line of study of *chaînes opératoires*. But the most interesting aspect of this turning point was the type of projects that started to appear.

In the early 1990s, the Portuguese archaeologists, both the "first" and "second generations", started to submit research proposals to different funding institutions. Of course, this fact also shows a development from the earlier decade, when there was no possibility for long-term research. This development was only partially a consequence of the American archaeologists in Portugal. These had impact only at the level of the government institute that coordinated archaeology, then the *Instituto Português de Património Arquitectónico e Arqueológico*. Although the law clearly stated that all excavations could only take place within a larger project, funding was still decided upon yearly.

It was a different state organism, the *Junta Nacional de Ciência e Tecnologia*, similar to the U.S. National Science Foundation, that made the first significant changes in research funding: the projects were now to be long-term, with a maximum of 4 years, and funding was to be decided upon for the whole length of the project. Of course, this organism changed science in Portugal, mostly due to the "hard" sciences such as Chemistry or Physics. This change occurred not only at the project level, but also at the individual Ph.D. grant level. Many individual grants were given to Portuguese students to finish doctoral degrees outside of Portugal, of which two were in Archaeology in American academic departments of Anthropology.

Those new archaeological projects concerned with the Paleolithic were not only designed for long-term research, but also included a diversity of specialists, ranging from zooarchaeologists to use-wear experts, and including special contracts with dating laboratories. This new model of project design is based on a multi- / inter- disciplinary perspective. The general tendency became to go further than just the single-site excavation. As a result, most projects focused on regional problems with diachronic characteristics, with long-term funding and large teams composed of a diversity of specialists.

The result of such efforts, paralleled by an increase in the number of known Paleolithic sites, paleoenvironmental data and absolute dates (there are now over 150 absolute dates for Portugal), is the change in what Clark (2001) calls conceptual frameworks or metaphysical paradigms. Of course, this change is only starting to be noted, and certainly mostly by those that "had the best of the two worlds", that is to say, a two-stage education: both in Portugal and in the US.

THE BEST OF TWO WORLDS

As a conclusion, one could say that the impact of American archaeology in the study of the Portuguese Upper Paleolithic, occurred at different levels. First, at the academic level, whereby American universities finished the education of a handful of Portuguese students, who are now in strategic positions, such as universities, research institutes or even (although not permanently) at the new state organism that regulates all archaeological work in Portugal, the *Instituto Português de Arqueologia*. At the same time, American Archaeology trained that group of people to think using different scientific paradigms. This, of course, resulted in long-term projects, with large

teams of different experts, with paleoecological problems in mind, as well as the study of site formation processes and taphonomic questions. The means of research funding also changed significantly. Money became an issue of importance, and both the first and second generations have learned where and how to obtain enough funding for their long-term projects. This fact is necessarily connected to the increase in quality, as observed by the international community, since, at least partially, those funds are now coming from international funding agencies. This aspect is again connected to a different scientific aspect of today's Portuguese Paleolithic archaeology; namely the amount of material published in languages other than Portuguese in edited volumes and international journals by those archaeologists. Naturally, these changes were related to new technologies and methodologies brought to Portugal and used as extensively as possible in research projects.

These various aspects are both a consequence and a cause of the second level of impact of American archaeology in Portugal. This is the change from a purely historical perspective on culture (that is to say, a taxonomic and ethnic concept of the so-called cultural traditions) to a mix between the historical approach found in the European prehistoric research tradition and the synchronic anthropological, "American" perspective. This is a multifaceted point of view or a new research paradigm that can be found among most, if not all, archaeologists studying the Paleolithic in Portugal. Probably, some of these ideas (and biases) may start moving in the opposite direction: from the Portuguese researchers to the American archaeologists still working in Portugal. In any case, this new set of paradigms, resulting from the meeting of two cultural and scientific traditions, is certainly what can be called the best of two worlds.

Finally, one last word. To those who may not yet have guessed, I am one of the Portuguese archaeologists who is the result of the meeting of these two worlds. My undergraduate training went through two stages. The first was based on the French methodological and theoretical paradigms; a second phase with the new generation of Portuguese archaeologists who chose to criticize the old traditional perspectives. Finally I saw- still as a student- the arrival of the American group. And, as you may have guessed again, I was one of the first students to go to US with a Portuguese grant for a Ph.D. degree. I had the opportunity to work in the field with all of the

American and Canadian archaeologists who went to Portugal. In some cases, I also worked in the lab with them, and in other cases I was also their student in the classroom. Most of them were on my Masters or Ph.D. committees. As a result, I did learn most of everything I know about Paleolithic archaeology with them: not only how to excavate, but also how to think about projects, funding, team composition, reaerch ethical aspects of the field, and many other things. However, I never forgot what I had learned in Portugal before I went to the U.S. And that information was what made me able to review and criticize everything I learned in the US.

The interesting aspect in all this is, clearly, the common notion, to both sides of the Atlantic that the difference resides not as much in the methodological world, but in the respective definitions of culture: on one side, a historical and diachronic perspective based on the notion of long standing cultural traditions, and on the other side, the short-term anthropological perspectives of cultural processes. These two confronting and almost antagonistic perspectives are the result of the cultural and paradigmatic biases of the societies & cultures where they were created. My bias is different from either one, since my culture and my education were impacted by both sides of the Atlantic. Hopefully, I was able to keep the best of the two worlds...

Departamento de História, Arqueologia e Património
Faculdade de Ciências Humanas e Sociais
Universidade do Algarve
Campus de Gambelas
8000 Faro, PORTUGAL
nbicho@ualg.pt

BIBLIOGRAPHY

ALMEIDA, F., 2000. *The Terminal Gravettian of Portuguese Estremadura: Ecological variability of the lithic industries*. Unpublished Ph.D. dissertation. Southern Methodist University, Dallas.

BICHO, N., 1992. *Technological Change in the Final Upper Paleolithic of Rio Maior, Portuguese Estremadura*. Ph.D. dissertation. Southern Methodist University, Dallas.

BREUIL, H., 1918. Impressions de voyage paléolithique à Lisbonne. *Terra Portuguesa* III, p. 34-39.

BREUIL, H. & ZBYSZEWSKI, G., 1942. Contribution à l'étude des industries paléolithiques du Portugal et de leurs rapports avec de la géologie du Quaternaire. *Comunicações dos Serviços Geológicos de Portugal* 23.

BREUIL, H. & ZBYSZEWSKI, G., 1946. Contribution á l'étude des industries paléolithiques des plages quaternaires de l'Alentejo littoral. *Comunicações dos Serviços Geologicos de Portugal* 27.

CLARK, G., 2001. Causes and Consequences of paradigmatic bias in French and American Upper Paleolithic archaeology. In *Pre-prints of the XIVth Congress of the UISPP*. ULg, Liège. p. 157.

DELGADO, J.F.N., 1867. *Da existência do homen em tempos mui remotos provada pelo estudo das cavernas. I – Notícia àcerca das grutas da Cesareda*. Lisboa, Comissão Geológica de Portugal.

GRAYSON, D., 1983. *The establishment of Human Antiquity*. Academic Press, New York.

GRAYSON, D., 1986. Eoliths, archaeological ambiguity, and the generation of "Middle-Range" research. In *American Archaeology. Past and Future*, edited by D. J. Meltzer, D. D. Fowler and A. Sabloff. Smithsonian Institution Press, Washington. p. 77-133.

HARROLD, F., 2001. Transatlantic Prehistory: The encounter between American and European Paleolithic Prehistory. In *Pre-prints of the XIVth Congress of the UISPP*. Liège. p. 155.

HELENO, M., 1956. Um quarto de século de investigação arqueológica. *O Arqueólogo Português* II-III, p. 221-237.

RAPOSO, L. & PENALVA, C., 1987. Uma colecção de Artefactos Mirenses do Vale da Telha (Aljezur). *Espaço Cultural,* Ano II, 2, p. 23-50.

RAPOSO, L., PENALVA, C. & PEREIRA, J.P., 1989. Notícia da descoberta da Estação Mirense de Palheirões do Alegra, Cabo Sardão (Odemira, Portugal). In *Actas da 2a Reunion del Cuaternario Iberico*, Madrid.

ROCHE, J., 1964. Le Paléolithique supérieur portugais. Bilan de nos connaissances et problèmes. *Bulletin de la Société Préhistorique Française* 31, p. 41-47.

ROCHE, J., 1977. Quelques indications sur le milieu de la province d'Estremadura (Portugal) au Pléistocène final. In *Approche écologique de l'homme fossile*. Supplément au Bulletin de l'Association Française pour l'Étude du Quaternaire 47. Bordeaux.

ROCHE, J., 1979. Le Magdalénien Portugais. In *La Fin des Temps Glaciaires en Europe*, edited by D. Sonneville-Bordes. Editons du CNRS, Paris. p. 753-758.

ROCHE, J., 1982. A gruta chamada Lapa do Suão (Bombarral). *Arqueologia* 5, p. 5-18.

ROCHE, J., & FERREIRA, O. 1970. Stratigraphie et faunes des niveaux paléolithiques de la Grotte de Salemas (Ponte de Lousa). *Comunicações dos Serviços Geológicos de Portugal*, 59, p. 253-263.

STRAUS, L., 2001. A (not quite) New Hampshire Yankee in the Abbé Breuil's court: reflections on my 30 years of Upper Paleolithic research in Atlantic Europe. In *Pre-prints of the XIVth Congress of the UISPP*. Ulg Liège. p. 154.

THACKER, P., 1996. *A Landscape Perspective on Upper Paleolithic Settlement in Portuguese Estremadura*. Unpublished Ph.D. dissertation. Southern Methodist University, Dallas.

VIERRA, B., 1992. *Subsistence Diversification and the Evolution of Microlithic Technologies: a study of the Portuguese Mesolithic*. Ph.D dissertation. University of New Mexico. Albuquerque.

ZILHÃO, J., 1993. As origens da Arqueologia Paleolítica em Portugal e a obra metodologicamente precursora de J.F. Nery Delgado. *Arqueologia e História*, Série 10, 3, p. 111-125.

ATTRIBUTE ANALYSIS AT THE ABRI PATAUD

Harvey M. BRICKER

Résumé: Le projet de fouilles à l'abri Pataud (Les Eyzies, Dordogne), mené par Hallam L. Movius Jr. de l'Université de Harvard, fut l'une des initiatives américaines les plus ambitieuses de l'étude du Paléolithique supérieur européen de la moitié du vingtième siècle. Pendant les années 1960, les étudiants du Prof. Movius tentèrent de développer de nouvelles méthodes d'analyse des industries lithiques abondantes par le biais de "l'analyse d'attributs". Ces tentatives étaient solidement ancrées dans l'archéologie anthropologique américaniste de l'époque - par exemple, le débat Ford-Spaulding à propos de la typologie, les opinions sur la "typologie" par opposition à la "classification", et un enthousiasme grandissant pour les statistiques de probabilité. Bien que quelques Européens adoptèrent la même approche analytique, les efforts de l'équipe de l'abri Pataud et d'autres américains (comme Sackett) suscitèrent peu d'intérêt et d'autant moins d'approbation en Europe. Dans leurs analyses des industries de Pataud, David, Clay, Bricker et Brooks tentèrent de montrer ce qui pouvait être accompli en n'adoptant pas une approche basée strictement sur une liste-type. Cependant, l'analyse d'attributs n'apporta pas ce qu'on en attendait, en grande partie parce qu'elle fut entreprise une décennie ou plus avant que la puissance des ordinateurs personnels ne permette d'effectuer, à moindre coût et plus facilement, les manipulations statistiques multivariées itératives requises. Le temps que la technologie informatique se mette en place, beaucoup d'entre nous, qui nous étions intéressés à de tels sujets, étions passés à d'autres intérêts dans d'autres domaines, et les préhistoriens européens poursuivaient des voies très différentes et plus axées sur la technologie. Le moment le plus propice était passé.

Abstract: The abri Pataud project, carried out in Les Eyzies (France) by Hallam L. Movius, Jr., of Harvard University, was one of the most ambitious American initiatives in the study of the European Upper Palaeolithic in the middle of the 20th century. Throughout the 1960s, his students tried to develop new ways of analyzing the abundant lithic industries through what was called «attribute analysis». These attempts were solidly grounded in Americanist anthropological archaeology of the day - for example, the Ford-Spaulding debate about the meaning of typology, views about «typology» vs «classification», and a growing enthusiasm for probability statistics. Although a few Europeans were working along similar lines, the efforts of the Pataud workers and other Americans (like Sackett) evoked little interest and even less approval in Europe. Through their analyses of the Pataud industries, David, Clay, Bricker, and Brooks attempted to show what could be achieved if one departed from a strictly type-list approach. However, the promise of attribute analysis was not realized, in large part because it was attempted a decade or more before the power of personal computers made the iterative multivariate statistical manipulations that are required both very cheap and very easy. By the time the computer technology arrived, many of us who had been interested in such matters had moved on to other interests in other areas, and European scholars had pursued very different, more technologically oriented avenues. The most opportune moment had passed.

The abri Pataud project, carried out in Les Eyzies (southwestern France) by Hallam L. Movius, Jr., of Harvard University (Movius 1974, 1975; Bricker 1995), was one of the most ambitious American initiatives in the study of the European Upper Palaeolithic in the middle of the 20th century. As has been noted by others (for example, Biberson 1979; Montet-White 1985), Movius sought to apply new excavation techniques to the problems of digging a rockshelter. Throughout the 1960s, his students, of whom I was one, tried to develop new ways of analyzing the abundant stone tool industries recovered. These latter attempts were grounded in the kind of Americanist archaeology all of us - Nicholas David, Berle Clay, Alison Brooks, and I - had encountered in our graduate training. One concept that was important to what we were doing then is a distinction between *classification* and *typology* made in the 1940s by an American archaeologist, Alex

Krieger (1944). Classification systems «...provide a series of pigeonholes into which specimens are sorted and then tabulated» (1944:273). Typology, on the other hand, aims to define «...a series of structural features which have proved historical significance. Determinative criteria are not of constant value, but are discovered as the material is analyzed...» (1944:273). The de Sonneville-Bordes/Perrot 92-type list (1954-1956) was a classification system, and it was an extremely useful one, which I used in all my work. Its goal was a different one from the one I was pursuing, but there was no conflict. It was a parallel universe - apples vs oranges

It was, however, another giant of American archaeology, Albert Spaulding, who began to show how true typology could be carried out by archaeologists. Spaulding (1953) showed how simple bivariate statistics could be used to demonstrate that

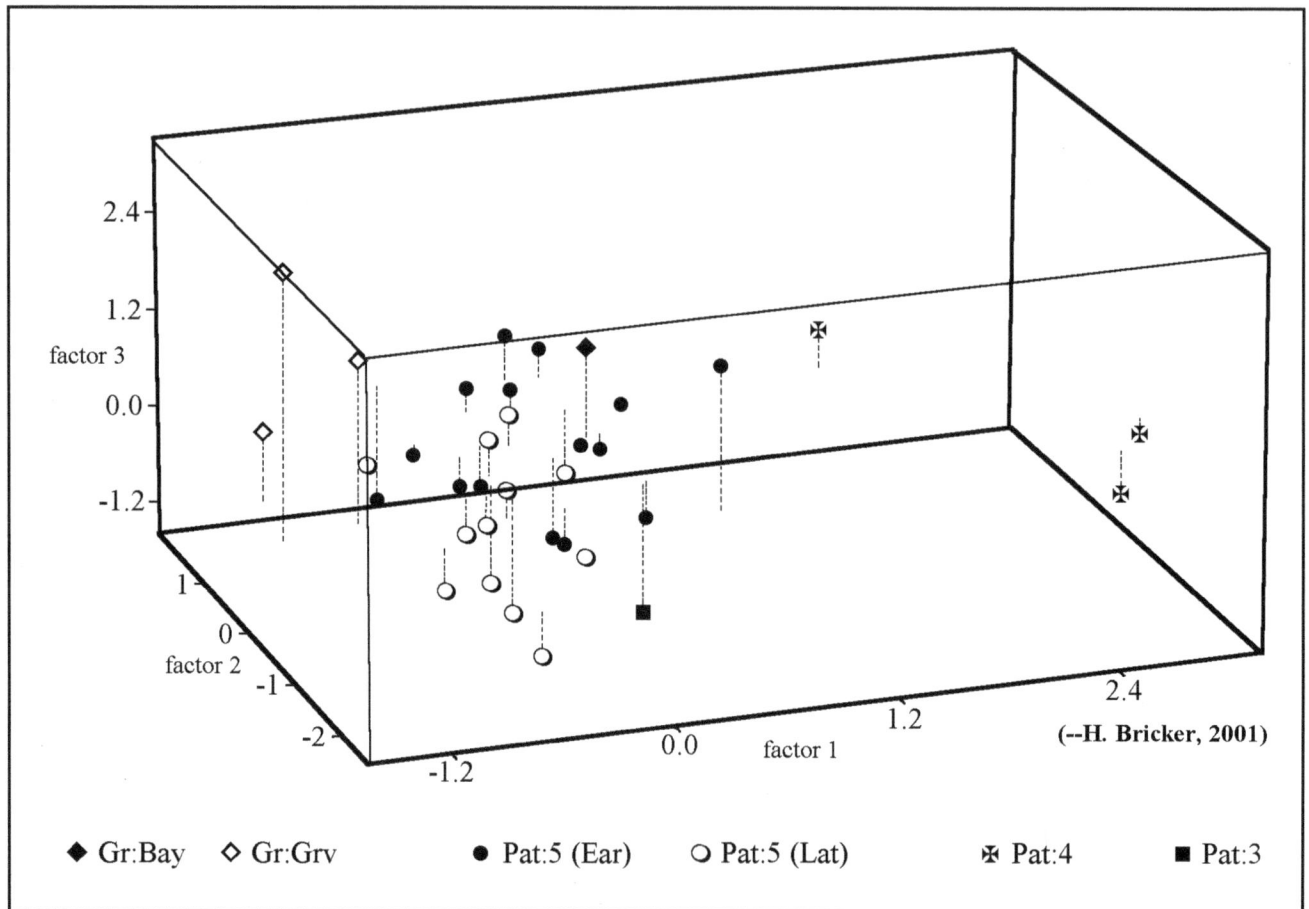

Figure 1. - Scatterplot of factor scores for 36 end-scraper samples from La Gravette and abri Pataud. Gr:Bay = the "Bayacian" level at La Gravette; Gr:Grv = the "Gravettian" levels (Jaune, Rouge, Noire) at La Gravette; Pat:(Ear) = the earlier units (FRONT:LOWER and FRONT:MIDDLE) of Level 5 at abri Pataud; Pat:5(Lat) = the later units (FRONT:UPPER and REAR) of Level 5 at abri Pataud; Pat:4 = Level 4 at abri Pataud; Pat:3 = Level 3 at abri Pataud.

combinations of attributes - attribute clusters and co-occurrences - were real, occurring in frequencies that surpassed chance. Spaulding's examples and his discussion of them showed also that what was really important for understanding the behavior of past artificers was the statistical demonstration of nonrandom attribute co-occurrence. This was more important than trying to use such co-occurrence to define rigid types - which, in any case, had demonstrated validity only in the assemblage under study. His work pointed toward the primary importance of *subtypological* analysis, which was the method we tried to develop for the analysis of Upper Palaeolithic assemblages.

Spaulding's work became part of a debate with James Ford about the reality of types in archaeological material. We thought Ford's point of view (for example, Ford 1954) was dead wrong, and in this we were in firm agreement with our French colleagues - for example, de Sonneville-Bordes (1966:4-5), in a sharply worded statement about some differences

between French and what she called Anglo-Saxon methodologies in prehistory. Despite this area of agreement, our enthusiasm for probability statistics had essentially *nothing* in common with what the French meant by "la méthode statistique". Here again it was a question of apples and oranges.

Through their analyses of the Pataud industries, David, Clay, Bricker, and Brooks attempted to show what could and should be done if one departed from a strictly type-list approach. Our subtypological approach to the study of artifacts was what we called "attribute analysis". Although some few Europeans were working along similar lines, the efforts of the Pataud workers and other Americans (like James Sackett [1966]) evoked little interest and even less approval in Europe. One European who was doing almost exactly the same thing we were but who had started a few years earlier was Lászlo Vértes (1964), in his analysis of the Tata Mousterian assemblages. We found out about this, however, only after our own work was underway.

Now, more than a quarter century later, I must conclude that our attempts to develop at the abri Pataud a new "attribute analysis" method for describing and comparing stone-tool assemblages can be seen to have essentially failed because these attempts were made ten years or so too soon, a decade or so before the power of personal computers made the iterative multivariate statistical manipulations required both very cheap and very easy. As a result, we could not use our analytical tools, which were themselves excellent, to anything like their full potential. The analysis of some end-scraper samples carried out by me and by Nicholas David can provide an example of what we did and what we failed to do.

The example of relevance here concerns 36 stratigraphically defined samples of end-scrapers - 4 from La Gravette, 28 from Level 5 at the abri Pataud (Pataud:5), 3 from Pataud:4, and 1 from Pataud:3 - that had been analyzed in terms of the standard attribute sets for end-scrapers used at the abri Pataud (Movius et al. 1968). These samples contained over 1500 scraping edges. Some results of the attribute analyses of these end-scrapers, done originally in the 1960s, were published in the 1970s and 1980s (for example, Bricker 1977:50; Bricker and David 1984; David 1985) and briefly summarized in later works (for example, chapters by David and Bricker in Bricker 1995). Some of the conclusions arrived at through these analyses were a) that the end-scrapers of the so-called Bayacian level of La Gravette were similar to those of the earlier units of Pataud:5; b) the end-scrapers of the later units of Pataud:5 were similar to both those of the "Gravettian" levels at La Gravette and those of Pataud:3; and c) that the Noaillian end-scrapers of Pataud:4 were quite different from those of Pataud:3, Pataud:5, or La Gravette. However, the documentation of these conclusions was cumbersome, based almost entirely on single-attribute frequency distributions and bivariate comparisons.

Reanalysis of the same data from the 36 samples was done more recently using 11 variables of the scraping edge, the blank, and the relationship of the former to the latter. (A detailed presentation of this reanalysis, which cannot be made in this brief communication, is planned for publication elsewhere.) A factor analysis produced scores, for each of the 36 samples, of the three factors with eigenvalues greater than 1.0. Plotting the factor scores in a 3D diagram produces the cluster shown in Figure 1. The distinctiveness of the Noaillian end-scrapers from Pataud:4 (particularly those from the

Middle and Upper units, the two most divergent symbols) can be seen at a glance, as can the close relationship between the end-scrapers of Pataud:5 and La Gravette. Unfortunately, such clear results of attribute analysis at the abri Pataud were not presented in the 1960s.

Because we could not easily cope with the necessary multivariate analyses at the appropriate time, the promise of attribute analysis at the abri Pataud was not realized. By the time the computer technology arrived, many of us who had been interested in such matters had moved on to other interests in other areas, and European scholars had pursued very different, more technologically oriented avenues. The two trains, American and European, had passed in the night.

Department of Anthropology
Tulane University
1021 Audubon Street
New Orleans, LA 70118
USA
hbricker@tulane.edu

BIBLIOGRAPHY

BIBERSON, P., 1979, [Review of] Excavation of the Abri Pataud, Les Eyzies (Dordogne), Stratigraphy, by H. L. Movius, Jr. *L'Anthropologie* 83, p. 318-319.

BRICKER, HARVEY M., 1977, La contribution de l'Abri Pataud à la question bayacienne. *Congrès Préhistorique de France*, C. R. de la XXe Session, Provence, 1974. Paris: S. P. F., p. 48-52.

BRICKER, HARVEY M., editor, 1995, *Le Paléolithique supérieur de l'abri Pataud (Dordogne): les fouilles de H. L. Movius Jr.* Paris: Editions de la Maison des Sciences de l'Homme.

BRICKER, HARVEY M. & DAVID, NICHOLAS, 1984, *Excavation of the Abri Pataud, Les Eyzies (Dordogne), The Périgordian VI (Level 3) Assemblage.* Cambridge: Peabody Museum.

DAVID, NICHOLAS, 1985, *Excavation of the Abri Pataud, Les Eyzies (Dordogne), The Noaillian (Level 4) Assemblages and the Noaillian Culture in Western Europe.* Cambridge: Peabody Museum.

FORD, JAMES A., 1954, On the concept of types. *American Anthropologist* 56, p. 42-57.

KRIEGER, ALEX D., 1944, The typological concept. *American Antiquity* 9, p. 271-288.

MONTET-WHITE, ANTA, 1985, [Review of] Excavation of the Abri Pataud, Les Eyzies (Dordogne) [first three volumes, published in 1975, 1977, and 1984], by H. L. Movius, Jr., et al. *Quarterly Review of Archaeology* 6(1), p. 5-6.

MOVIUS, HALLAM L., JR., 1974, The Abri Pataud program of the French Upper Palaeolithic in retrospect. In *Archaeological Researches in Retrospect,* edited by G. R. Willey. Cambridge: Winthrop Publishers.

MOVIUS, HALLAM L., JR., editor, 1975, *Excavation of the Abri Pataud, Les Eyzies (Dordogne).* Cambridge: Peabody Museum.

MOVIUS, HALLAM L., JR., DAVID, NICHOLAS C., BRICKER, HARVEY M., & CLAY, R. BERLE, 1968, *The Analysis of Certain Major Classes of Upper Palaeolithic Tools.* Cambridge: Peabody Museum.

SACKETT, JAMES R., 1966, Quantitative analysis of Upper Palaeolithic stone tools. *American Anthropologist* 68 (no. 2, pt. 2), p. 356-394.

SONNEVILLE-BORDES, DENISE DE, 1966, L'évolution du Paléolithique supérieur en Europe Occidentale et sa signification. *Bulletin de la Société Préhistorique Française* 63, p. 3-34.

SONNEVILLE-BORDES, DENISE DE & PERROT, JEAN, 1954-1956, Lexique typologique du Paléolithique supérieur. *Bulletin de la Société Préhistorique Française* 51, p. 327-335; 52, p. 76-79; 53, p. 408-412, 547-559.

SPAULDING, ALBERT C., 1953, Statistical techniques for the discovery of artifact types. *American Antiquity* 18, p. 305-313.

VERTES, LASZLO, 1964, *Tata: Eine Mittelpaläolithische Travertin-Siedlung in Ungarn.* Budapest: Akadémiai Kiadó.

OBSERVATIONS ON PARADIGMATIC BIAS IN FRENCH AND AMERICAN PALEOLITHIC ARCHAEOLOGY

Geoffrey A. CLARK

Résumé: Les préhistoriens n'articulent que rarement de façon explicite les cadres conceptuels (ou paradigmes métaphysiques) qui sous-tendent la formulation de déductions logiques dans leurs traditions de recherche nationales et/ou régionales. Cette situation est fort problématique puisqu'au point de vue interprétatif, ces paradigmes diffèrent souvent entre eux de façon marquée, sans toutefois que ces divergences ne soient nécessairement évidentes aux divers chercheurs qui les emploient.

Dans le contexte de sa tradition d'origine, un paradigme est toujours conséquent, de telle sorte qu'il existe généralement chez les chercheurs issus d'une même tradition un consensus relatif aux types d'explications considérées a priori comme acceptables. Cependant, comme les assomptions qui sous-tendent le métaphysique influencent nécessairement la nature des paradigmes subordonnés, lorsque la recherche paléolithique implique plus d'une tradition intellectuelle, des conflits peuvent survenir à propos des types d'explications considérées comme plausibles. Ces différences implicites ont pour effet de confondre l'identification de modalités de comportement préhistorique et la potentielle signification des modèles comportementaux tels qu'identifiés archéologiquement.

Dans cet essai, l'auteur trace les grands traits des paradigmes métaphysiques français et américains et identifie certaines des préconceptions, préjugés et assomptions de la tradition de recherche française qui sont problématiques d'une perspective américaine. Bien que le développement de la « middle range theory » (ex., Binford 1981) soit fort important, les biais interprétatifs imposés par le métaphysique influencent toute interprétation archéologique et ce, quel que soit son niveau d'abstraction.

Abstract: Because they are seldom made explicit, the conceptual frameworks (or metaphysical paradigms) that structure the logic of inference in the various national and regional research traditions involved in Paleolithic archaeology can differ profoundly from one another in ways that are not always obvious, or immediately apparent - even to those doing the work. Paradigms are logically consistent within research traditions and there is usually a consensus about the kinds of explanations regarded, a priori, as plausible or not. However, because the assumptions underlying the metaphysic determine the character of lower order paradigms, when more than one intellectual tradition is involved, conflicts can arise in respect of the nature of explanation and what kinds of explanations are regarded as plausible or not. These implicit differences have far-reaching consequences for construals of pattern, and what pattern might mean. This paper outlines the metaphysical paradigms of French and American archaeology, and identifies some of the biases, preconceptions and assumptions in the French research tradition that appear problematic from an American point of view. While the development of middle range theory is clearly appropriate and important (e.g., Binford 1981), implicit bias at the level of the metaphysic influences interpretation of all aspects of archaeological research, and at every level.

WHY EPISTEMOLOGY IS IMPORTANT

As I have argued for a long time now, if we are to reduce the amount of miscommunication in Paleolithic archaeology, and increase the ratio of information to noise, we have an obligation to tell people where we're coming from in terms of our conceptual frameworks. We must confront directly the fundamental ambiguity which is so much a part of any archaeological record anywhere, and try to make explicit the inferential basis for knowledge claims in the areas and problem domains in which we work. The Upper Paleolithic is a good example of this. It's a multidisciplinary, multinational endeavor, and the conceptual frameworks used by various workers can differ profoundly from one another in ways that are not immediately apparent, even to those engaged in the research.

As an American working in the Old World Paleolithic for more than three decades, I've noticed a couple things about what - for lack of a better term - I'd call epistemology (how we know what we think we know about the remote past). One was that archeologists are assiduous 'pattern searchers', but they usually don't worry very much about how they go about this search. They tend to adopt the prevailing systematics of the research tradition in which they were trained, and proceed pretty much on the assumption that those systematics are adequate to the task at hand. This means that the logic of inference is seldom examined in an explicit way, and that in consequence people tend to 'talk past' one another. Proceeding from different biases and preconceptions about the human past, and defining differently terms and concepts thought to be held in common, they often don't understand what their colleagues are talking about.

Thinking about these things, it occurred to me that - before we can build strong inference - it's first necessary to examine the existing logic of inference in order to be able to understand what it does well, and what it does poorly. A concern with inferential logic is not a strong suit of Paleolithic research, which tends to be methodologically obsessive, 'discovery' and 'data' driven, and dominated by 'strict empiricists' - people who think that pattern is latent in nature, that it's easily accessible to the prepared mind and, in some extreme cases, that 'the facts speak for themselves'.

Suffice it to say I don't think 'the facts speak for themselves'; I don't think pattern is latent in nature, merely awaiting discovery, and so forth. I do think that pattern or structure is imposed, to a very considerable extent, on nature by humans, and that data don't exist independent of the conceptual frameworks that define them. What exists independent of our conceptual frameworks are stones and bones in ancient geological contexts, but they don't constitute data until they are observed and measured and classified according to investigator-derived schemata. It is how we go about doing this that makes our inferences strong or weak, naïve or sophisticated.

To argue for an explicit concern with the logic of inference in archaeology is nothing new; it was a cornerstone of the Americanist processual approach of the mid-1960s (e.g., Binford 1965, Clarke 1972). However, I suggest that processualism has had relatively little impact on Paleolithic archaeology, especially as practiced by Old World workers, and that epistemological angst is mostly confined to the anglophone research traditions. Proceeding from a natural science paradigm, many Latin European

prehistorians treat the archaeological record as if it were directly analogous to that of paleontology or geology, with type sites, sequences, and index fossils that supposedly embody the full range of variation expected in the material remains of what are often taken to be extinct 'cultures'. Underlying this view is the preconception that prehistory is history projected back into the preliterate past, and that process in 'deep time' can be treated as analogous to, and an extension of, process in recent historical contexts (Clark & Lindly 1991, Clark 1993).

From a philosophical point of view, of course, one metaphysical paradigm is 'as good as another' (i.e., its internal logic is consistent, its explanations coherent and adequate given that logic). But, because the assumptions underlying the metaphysic determine the character of its subordinate paradigms (which in turn determine research protocols in any problem context), conflicts often arise in respect of the nature of explanation, and what kinds of explanations are regarded as plausible or not. These problems are exacerbated in Upper Paleolithic research, which is of interest and importance to several quite different intellectual traditions. From an American perspective, there are big problems with the contention that prehistory is an extension of history, and these have far-reaching implications for some European construals of pattern, and what it might mean.

OLD AND NEW WORLD ARCHAEOLOGICAL RESEARCH TRADITIONS

Let's try to get a little more specific about these questions of implicit bias at the level of the metaphysic. Table 1 shows the major tenets of the Old and New World archaeological research traditions in respect of the central concept of 'culture' (Binford & Sabloff 1982). In the New World (or, more accurately, the anglophone New World), the conception of culture adopted by archaeologists originated in culture area studies, and was developed principally by cultural anthropologists at Berkeley and Columbia beginning in the 1920s. This notion of culture was characterized by the presumption of much continuity across extensive geographical areas, manifest in the form and distribution of its material residues. Cultures were also perceived to be very stable in space and time, at least so long as the natural environment didn't change very much. Marked discontinuities in pattern were regarded as exceptional. Finally, culture was cohesive so far as its characteristics or traits were concerned, and was thought to exist *above* the level of the identity-conscious social units that produced those traits. In my opinion, this was, and remains, the most important distinction between the Old and the New World paradigms, especially as they bear on the assignment of meaning to pattern in Paleolithic archaeology.

In the Old World, culture was often considered to be the material expression of distinct ethnic or social groups analogous to those known from history or ethnography, so it existed *at the level* of such groups, and not above them. Such groups were also thought to be coherent, fixed, bounded in time and space, and relatively changeless. A given archaeological assemblage thus tended to be equated with a given identity-conscious social unit, although this equation was seldom made explicit. Cultures were seen (and, in my opinion, continue to be seen) as packages of traits differentiated amongst themselves, but not differentiated internally.

These two conceptions of culture are metaphysical paradigms recapitulating expectations about what culture is 'like'. Both are based on empirical generalizations, but they proceed from different sets of implicit assumptions about pattern and what it might mean. Both consist of attempts to describe the material referents of culture, but given that the two notions of culture are different, the descriptions and explanations of the patterns perceived in each case are also different. The New World paradigm provides us with a portrait of geographical and temporal continuity, but it is a limited kind of continuity in comparison with the time-space framework of the Old World. Moreover, the New World paradigm views the archaeological record, almost inevitably, as a series of births and growths, followed by a series of collapses or declines, and the cycle is repeated over and over again.

The Old World paradigm provides us with an ideational portrait of culture in which archaeological assemblages are equated with distinct, identity-conscious social units of some kind. It's a view of culture characterized by a *lack of continuity* across time - by a series of time-successive replacements - and also by a lack of geographical continuity, each culture being defined spatially by its own assemblage of 'diagnostic' artifacts. There are also differences of scale. Cultures are seen as immutable over the long term, and when there are changes (and they are rare), they tend to be abrupt and complete, and are usually

explained by the physical replacement of one group by another. In general, cultures in the Old World paradigm change less, mix less, and are modified only gradually, if at all, over the course of time. It's a model characterized by a kind of punctuated equilibrium, with long periods of stasis corresponding to the classic, prehistorian-defined analytical units, 'punctuated' by transition episodes of relatively short duration, which coincide with unit boundaries.

The Old World paradigm is also characterized by certain other tendencies which seem problematic from an American perspective. One is the longstanding European tendency to emphasize typological systematics to the near exclusion of other lines of evidence, as if retouched stone artifacts were in some way intrinsically meaningful (or more meaningful than other categories of data). A post-1985 shift toward more emphasis on the organization of technology has mitigated this problem to some extent, although technological patterns are frequently explained in exactly the same ways as typological ones - by invoking 'traditions' transmitted by social learning in the context of hypothetical identity-conscious social units that persist unchanged over tens of millennia and hundreds of thousands of square kilometers (e.g., Goren-Inbar et al. 2000). There are big problems with this.

A second bias that appears problematic from an American point of view is the tendency for European Paleolithic archaeologists to overlook the fact that what shows up archaeologically is not so much an inventory of tool complexes preserved intact as a "landscape of lithic discard", as Jim Sackett put it, consisting of the exhausted, worn out, broken, and laterally recycled remains of multi-component 'general-purpose' tools, designed for use in a wide variety of contexts (Sackett 1988). These observations underscore the European tendency to place too much emphasis on the artifacts themselves, and to study artifacts as a domain of investigation isolated from other such domains.

Finally, and in keeping with its natural science origins, there is a strong European commitment to *multidisciplinary* research, but this is accompanied by what Americans sometimes perceive to be a rather puzzling de-emphasis on *interdisciplinary* integration of research conclusions. This goes along with a near-total lack of 'landscape archaeology', insufficient emphasis on the geographical and environmental settings of sites, and a tendency to extract the site from its social and natural context

Table 1: Metaphysical Paradigms in Prehistoric Archaeology - Biases and Preconceptions of the Anglophone New World and the Latin Old World Conceptions of Culture (Binford & Sabloff 1982, Clark 1993).

New World Paradigm	Old World Paradigm
The definition of culture	
Developed out of culture area studies	Developed out of European history and nationalism
Received its mandate from cultural anthropology	Received its mandate from natural science (esp. geology, paleontology)
Essentially gradualist, emphasized continuity over space and time	Characterized by punctuated equilibrium; emphasized discontinuity in that aspects of material culture were believed to correspond to relatively discrete 0posocial, ethnic, linguistic groups
Led to normative (i.e., variety-minimizing) views of culture manifest in diagnostic artifact types (e.g., projectile points)	Also normative; cultures equated with differentiated packages of diagnostic traits (i.e., archaeological index fossils)
Recognizes some vectored change within temporally and spatially large and vaguely defined analytical units	Essentially static within equally large and vague analytical units
Coherent; cultures equated with trait complexes that cohere over space and time unless or until the physical environment changes	Incoherent; when cultures changed, they changed *en bloc* and relatively abruptly; the principle cause of culture change is population replacement
Culture exists at a level *above* that of social, ethnic, and linguistic groups	Culture exists *at the level* of social, ethnic, and linguistic groups
Social organization, ethnicity, and language vary independently of one another	Social organization, ethnicity, and language covary more or less directly with one another
Many definitions of culture; some ideational, others phenomenological	Definition of culture essentially ideational - culture comprises a monothetic set of norms, values in people's heads which are manifest in their material remains

and consider it as the principal analytical unit. Put another way, the research traditions of Latin Europe appear to lack a systemic perspective of sufficiently broad scope to facilitate analysis of multiple variables and patterns simultaneously. The Latin European preoccupation with artifact typology, and with site- and sequence-centered archaeology, sometimes distracts European prehistorians from what Americans would regard as other, more productive lines of investigation (e.g., technological organization, raw material procurement, use and discard patterns; intrasite spatial analysis, settlement pattern studies, etc.). However, the absence of an integrative, systemic approach to the study of changing human adaptation, a reluctance to examine the logic of inference underlying knowledge claims, and a failure to identify an explicit conceptual framework by which meaning might be assigned to pattern are perhaps the biggest points of departure between the intellectual traditions in the two regions.

THE MIDDLE-UPPER PALEOLITHIC TRANSITION

Table 2 shows the criteria frequently used in Europe to define the appearance of the Upper Paleolithic. These criteria, which have become widely disseminated 'textbook generalizations', are ultimately derived from a package of preconceptions and biases expressed through typological systematics that, while completely consilient with the European paradigm, are nevertheless problematic from an American standpoint. The Upper Paleolithic typology has not come under the same intense scrutiny as that of the Middle Paleolithic. This is probably because, in the days before radiocarbon dates were widely available, the typology was apparently very successful at partitioning the industries of the Upper Paleolithic by using an index fossil-based system of time-sensitive 'stylistic' marker types. More recently,

Table 2: Behavioral Changes and Their Material Correlates that Supposedly Accompany the Middle-Upper Paleolithic Transition in Europe (e.g., Mellars 1989a, Tattersall 1998).

(1) A general shift in the pattern of stone tool technology from predominantly 'flake' technologies to more regular, standardized 'blade' technologies, achieved by means of more economical techniques of core preparation.

(2) A simultaneous increase in the variety and complexity of stone tools involving more standardization of shape, and a higher degree of 'imposed form' in the various stages of production.

(3) The appearance of relatively complex and extensively shaped bone, antler and ivory artifacts.

(4) An increase in the tempo of technological change (apparent both in lithic and in bone technology), accompanied by increased regional diversification of tool forms produced in different geographical areas.

(5) The appearance of wide range of beads, pendants, and other 'personal ornaments' made from perforated animal teeth and marine shells, and from more elaborately shaped bone, stone and ivory blanks.

(6) The appearance of sophisticated and highly complex forms of representational or 'naturalistic' art.

(7) Associated changes in both the economic and social organization of human groups, marked by (i) a much more specialized pattern of animal exploitation, based on systematic hunting, as opposed to opportunistic scavenging of game, (ii) a sharp increase in the overall density of human population, (iii) an apparent increase in the maximum size of local residential groups, and (iv) the appearance of more highly 'structured' sites, including more evidence for features (e.g., well-defined hearths, pits; huts, tents, and other habitations).

however, archaeologists have come to realize that there are problems with the general chronological order implied by this typology, and its original strength has become its greatest weakness, in that it 'weights' these index types much more heavily than it does other assemblage characteristics. A concentration on archaeological index fossils masks a great deal of variability within and between the traditional Upper Paleolithic analytical units. While many Europeans would acknowledge the possibility that there might be functional explanations for assemblage variability *within* conventionally-defined units like the Perigordian and the Aurignacian, for the most part they continue to reject the possibility that these units might themselves signify functional aspects of the same UP adaptations. Most European workers also assume that the Upper Paleolithic typologies monitor technology in some fairly direct way. Work in the Levant has shown that this is simply not the case (Marks 1983). In other words, typology and technology can, and do, vary independently of each another.

While lip service continues to be paid to these 'textbook generalizations', enshrined now in the literature for more than three decades as if they were 'facts,' how well are they actually supported empirically? For one thing, UP typological variation by no means consistently displays a high degree of formal standardization, nor do the types themselves segregate clearly and unambiguously. In fact, in some assemblages, the amount of intergradation between types is so great as to frustrate even the most experienced typologist, which suggests that the types (and perhaps even the type groups) might represent no more than modal points along a continuum of morphological variation (Sackett 1988, Clark 1999, Bisson 2000).

A second point is that, like their Mousterian counterparts, there is no reason to think that UP tools were not heavily subjected to modification over the course of their use-lives by continual use, breakage, subsequent rejuvenation and/or intentional reworking. This means that continual formal transformation is likely the rule, rather than the exception; that there might not be much design specificity in either the Middle or the Upper Paleolithic, and that Dibble's arguments about equifinality in the form of Mousterian sidescrapers (e.g., 1995) could apply with equal cogency to virtually all UP tool types, including the *fossiles directeurs*.

Finally, of the 92 types recognized in a conventional Bordesian UP type list, most sites actually contain relatively few of them, suggesting that what are perceived by archaeologists to be discrete types more often than not simply represent successive stages in the modification of a single generalized tool and/or minor alterations in form primarily determined by variations in blank morphology. The implication of this is that many (most) Upper Paleolithic retouched tool inventories are not more complex than their Middle Paleolithic counterparts, nor do they conform to more rigorous design specifications, nor are they more functionally specific - considerations that all but erase the supposed cognitive differences between the hominids that produced them.

QUESTIONING CONVENTIONAL WISDOM

Rather than taking their adequacy for granted, we need to directly confront the very real possibility that the existing systematics might not be up to the task of answering many questions deemed important by both research traditions (Clark 1997). We can begin by asking: What *are* the conventional archaeological analytical units (e.g., Châtelperronian, Aurignacian)? (see Straus 1987)? What do they mean, or represent, in behavioral terms? Why do we use them? Is there an explicit justification for using them? Are there alternatives? Are they demonstrably 'cultural' in any meaningful sense of the term, in that they can be shown to be the material remains of identity-conscious social units of some kind? If they are, how can we show that they are? If they are not, what are the implications of that for construals of pattern in the Paleolithic archaeological record? Whatever they are, are they 'the same thing' in western Europe? eastern Europe? south-central Europe? the Levant? Is it realistic or defensible to treat the analytical units as if they were quasi-historical entities, analogous to the social, ethnic and linguistic groups known to us from history? More generally, is it justifiable to treat process in 'deep time' (i.e., the Pleistocene) as if it were analogous to process in more recent historical contexts? If they are 'assemblage types' or 'technocomplexes' (*sensu* Clarke 1968), what is the mode of transmission through time, across space? What effects might the formal convergence that is so much a part of all lithic reduction have on assessments of the mode of transmission? What happens to the analytical units if technology is decoupled from typology (i.e., if typology is shown to vary independently of technology)? What are some of the implications that this might have for the conventional notion that typology and technology are related to one another in a regular and systematic way? What are the implications of a 'type site' or 'type assemblage'-based systematics as, for example, Tabun in Israel, K'sar Akil in Lebanon, or Combe Grenal and Laugerie Haute in France? Is it reasonable to expect that any site - no matter how long and well-dated its sequence of industries - would have any

generalizable properties whatsoever? Why should we expect it to? What does the evidence for planning depth, structured use of space, the construction of shelters, technological sophistication, economically-rational behavior, blade industries, and evidence for ritual and burials imply about human cognitive evolution when 'modern' patterns show up in 'pre-modern' contexts associated, in some cases, with 'pre-modern' hominids?

I suggest that the answers to these questions are of crucial importance to a better understanding of how we think about Paleolithic archaeological evidence. It is a facile assumption of those who have faith in the adequacy of the existing systematics that we are discovering, via retouched stone artifact typology, something very like the remains of identity-conscious social units analogous to the tribes, peoples and nations of history. To many Latin European workers, Paleolithic archaeology is essentially history projected back into the Pleistocene, and patterns are typically explained post-hoc by invoking processes (e.g., migrations) analogous to those operating in recent historical contexts. The whole approach is predicated on (1) the existence of tool making 'traditions' manifest in artifact form that are detectable over hundreds of thousands (even millions) of square kilometers; (2) the idea that such 'traditions' (ways of making stone tools transmitted in a social context from one generation to the next) persisted unchanged and intact over tens (or, in the case of the Lower Paleolithic, hundreds) of millennia, and (3) the conviction that they are detectable at points in space (e.g., Europe, the Levant) separated by thousands of kilometers.

I have argued at length that this paradigm, while internally consistent in respect of its logic of inference, cannot be reconciled with an Americanist perspective, and (1) that most of the Upper Paleolithic 'index fossil' tool types are ubiquitous (or nearly so), at least in western Eurasia, and carry little temporal and probably no social information whatsoever; (2) that there is only a minimal and generalized learned behavioral component to chipped stone artifact form, (3) that there is an enormous amount of equifinality in the (few) processes by which humans chip stone (i.e., much formal convergence conditioned by contextual factors - technology, raw material quality, size, distribution in the landscape, especially as affected by mobility; and (4) that this formal convergence almost certainly overrides (because of context, rock fracture mechanics) any hypothetical 'cultural' component. As Bordes himself once remarked, the widespread convergence of form in the Paleolithic is a consequence of repeated combinations of these relatively few factors (1968). While the pattern similarities themselves are uncontested, what is supposedly causing them to occur (historical connectivity over vast geographical areas and time ranges) is deeply problematic. It is possible to explain pattern similarities in Paleolithic archaeological assemblages without recourse to typology-based tool-making traditions. I make two points.

EXPLAINING PATTERN WITHOUT INVOKING HISTORY

First, there are serious logical and conceptual problems with the notion of a cultural component in the form of (most) Paleolithic artifacts. For one thing, the time-space distributions of prehistorian-defined analytical units (e.g., the Aurignacian) *exceed by orders of magnitude* the time-space distributions of any real or imaginable social entity that might have produced and transmitted them. Unless one resorts to essentialism (e.g., there is an ineffable 'Aurignacianness' manifest in the appearance of, e.g., Dufour bladelets), there is simply no behavioral or cultural mechanism whereby a hypothetical tool-making tradition could have been transmitted over thousands of years and millions of square kilometers. Thus, something other than historical connectivity must account for pattern similarities. For another, we have no guarantees that the basic analytical units themselves are discrete in space and time, are 'the same thing' whenever and wherever they are found. In fact, it is highly likely that they are not. The Aurignacian is, in fact, the quintessential illustration of this problem. The French Aurignacian is defined typologically by the presence of carinate endscrapers, blades, blades with scalar retouch ('Aurignacian blades'), strangled blades, Dufour bladelets, split-based bone points, bone and antler *sagaies,* etc., as well as by a range of non-lithic criteria (e.g., ornaments, portable and parietal art, 'well-organized' campsites, etc.). The Levantine Aurignacian is a flake industry bearing no resemblance whatsoever to its French counterpart. It almost entirely lacks personal ornaments, bone or antler tools, figurines, portable art in general, parietal art, burials, and 'well-organized' campsites, and, when these features of 'Aurignacianness' do appear together as a package, it is only in the later phases of the Epipaleolithic, in the Natufian, after c. 12 kyr ago (Marks 1994). Apart

from the occasional appearance of carinated tools in a few Levantine Aurignacian levels (e.g., K'sar Akil, Level 13), the only similarity between the French and the Levantine Aurignacians is the name itself, imported from France by several generations of Levantine scholars trained in the francophone tradition. So, whatever the Aurignacian is, it is manifestly not a 'culture' or a 'tradition'. I suggest that there is, in fact, no consensus on what the Aurignacian is (i.e., what, if anything, it represents behaviorally). The same can be said of all of the other prehistorian-defined Paleolithic analytical units. As Binford and Sabloff (1982) pointed out long ago, we need to confront this issue directly.

Second, there is the question of resolution and its consequences for identifying a tradition 'on the ground.' No known Paleolithic site sequence, or series of site sequences, is anywhere near fine-grained enough to allow us to identify the remains of the hypothetical social units that would have been the bearers of these lithic 'traditions' (i.e., assemblage resolution, integrity are far too low). Moreover, the generally-acknowledged fluidity of forager territorial boundaries would, in short order, have impossibly confounded any stylistic patterns that might have been manifest in stone tool form in the archaeological context. So, even if there were a 'cultural' component to the form of stone artifacts, we couldn't possibly detect it. It is not enough to claim, as some have done, that we cannot yet model 'Paleoculture' adequately. In fact, we can model it very well. By invoking identity-conscious 'migrants' whose peregrinations are supposedly manifest in timeless, changeless tool-making traditions, process in the remote past is treated as if it were analogous to process in recent historical contexts. While this is a perfectly reasonable thing to do from the perspective of many Latin European prehistorians, it makes no sense at all from the standpoint of Americanist anthropological archeology.

What we think of as Paleolithic technology almost certainly constituted a range of options very broadly distributed in time and space, held in common by all contemporary hominids, and invoked differentially according to context. The challenge of future work is to determine what contextual factors constrained choice amongst these options. Such factors probably include range and size of and distance to raw materials, forager mobility strategies (a consequence of resource distributions), anticipated tasks, group size and composition (which change seasonally, annually, generationally), structural pose of the occupants of a site in an annual round and, more generally, simply the duration of site occupation.

EPILOGUE

Like much paleoanthropology, Upper Paleolithic research tends to be 'discovery driven', obsessed with methodology, riddled with implicit bias, dominated by strict empiricism, and by essentialist, typological thinking about human biological and cultural variation (Clark 2000). While one could argue that, given enough pattern searching, we will eventually figure it all out, I don't think that's likely to happen because of the effects of implicit bias, because most workers feel no obligation whatsoever to make bias explicit, and because there is little or no concern with the logic of inference underlying knowledge claims in many sectors of the discipline. Inference is, therefore, typically rather weak, unrelated to an identifiable conceptual framework, and unsupported by warranting arguments of any kind. I think we can do better than this. To me, all good science is critically self-conscious science (to use David Clarke's [1973] memorable phrase). An explicit concern with epistemology cannot fail to result in a better, stronger, more credible Paleolithic archaeology.

Department of Anthropology
Arizona State University
Tempe, AZ 85287-2402
U.S.A.
e-mail: *gaclark@asu.edu*

BIBLIOGRAPHY

BINFORD, L., 1965, Archaeological systematics and the study of culture process. *American Antiquity* 31, p. 203-210.

BINFORD, L., 1981, Middle-range research and the role of actualistic studies. In *Bones: Ancient Men and Modern Myths.* New York: Academic Press, p. 21-30.

BINFORD, L. & SABLOFF, J., 1982, Paradigms, systematics, and archaeology. *Journal of Anthropological Research* 38, p. 137-152.

BISSON, M., 2000, Nineteenth-century tools for twenty-first century archaeology? Why the Middle Paleolithic typology of François Bordes must be replaced. *Journal of Archaeological Method and Theory* 7, p. 1-48.

BORDES, F., 1968, *The Old Stone Age.* New York: McGraw-Hill.

CLARK, G.A., 1993, Paradigms in science and archaeology. *Journal of Archaeological Research* 1, p. 203-234.

CLARK, G.A., 1997, The Middle-Upper Paleolithic transition in Europe: an American perspective. *Norwegian Archaeological Journal* 30, p. 25-53.

CLARK, G.A., 1999, Modern human origins: highly visible, curiously intangible. *Science* 283, p. 2029-2032; 284, p. 917.

CLARK, G. A., 2000, On the questionable practice of invoking the metaphysic. *American Anthropologist* 102, p. 851-853.

CLARK, G. & LINDLY, J., 1991, Paradigmatic biases and Paleolithic research traditions. *Current Anthropology* 32, p. 577-587.

CLARKE, D., 1968, *Analytical Archaeology.* London: Methuen.

CLARKE, D., 1972, Models and paradigms in contemporary archaeology. In *Models in Archaeology,* edited by D. Clarke. London: Methuen, p. 1-60.

CLARKE, D., 1973, Archaeology: the loss of innocence. *Antiquity* 47, p. 6-18.

DIBBLE, H., 1995, Middle Paleolithic scraper reduction: background, clarification, and review of the evidence to date. *Journal of Archaeological Method and Theory* 2, p. 299-368.

GOREN-INBAR, N., *et al.,* 2000, Pleistocene milestones on the out-of-Africa corridor at Gesher Benot Ya'aqov, Israel. *Science* 289, p. 944-947.

MARKS, A.E., 1983, The Middle-to-Upper Paleolithic transition in the Levant. *Advances in World Archaeology* 2, p. 51-98.

MARKS, A.E., 1994, In search of the Neandertals - a Levantine perspective. *Cambridge Archaeological Journal* 4, p. 104-106.

MELLARS, P., 1989, Major issues in he emergence of modern humans. *Current Anthropology* 30, p. 349-385.

SACKETT, J., 1988, The Mousterian and its aftermath: a view from the Upper Paleolithic. In *Upper Pleistocene Prehistory in Western Eurasia,* edited by H. Dibble & A. Montet-White. Philadelphia: University of Pennsylvania Museum Monograph No. 54, p. 413-426.

STRAUS, L., 1987, Paradigm lost? a personal view of the current state of Upper Paleolithic research. *Helinium* 27: 157-171.

TATTERSALL, I., 1998, *Becoming Human.* New York: Harcourt-Brace.

TRANSATLANTIC PREHISTORY: THOUGHTS ON THE ENCOUNTER BETWEEN AMERICAN AND EUROPEAN PALEOLITHIC PREHISTORY

Francis B. HARROLD

Résumé: Il y a eu relativement peu de recherche américaine significative sur le Paléolithique supérieur européen avant la deuxième moitié du 20ième siècle. Cet engagement s'est accru juste au moment où la "Nouvelle Archéologie" s'est dévelopée et ce fait a eu l'effet de contraster plus nettement les perspectives théoriques des préhistoriens européens et américains. Néanmoins et en dépit des désaccords persistants (surtout plus importants au niveau théorique que dans la méthodologie de fouille ou d'analyses au laboratoire), bien des échanges intellectuels d'intérêt mutuel ont eu lieu et continuent à ce jour. Si on pourrait dire une fois qu'il y ait eu des confrontations paradigmatiques absolues dans le passé, ce n'est plus le cas aujourd'hui. Les différents points de vue sur le sort des Néandertaliens et sur la transition entre le Paléolithique moyen et supérieur en Europe démontrent la manque d'une dichotomie sur des lignes strictement transatlantiques.

Abstract: Significant American involvement in European Paleolithic research did not occur until the second half of the twentieth century. This involvement accelerated at a time when such American developments as the "New Archaeology" accentuated contrasts in theoretical perspectives between European and U.S. prehistorians. Yet, despite some continuing disagreements (which are more important at the theoretical level than in field or laboratory methodology), much mutually beneficial intellectual exchange has occurred. If it could ever have been said that European-American interchange involved the clash between two incommensurable paradigms, it is not so today. The complex set of views concerning the fate of the Neanderthals and the Middle-Upper Paleolithic transition in Europe illustrates the lack of a European-American theoretical dichotomy.

The subject of the work by American archaeologists in the Paleolithic of Europe is a broad one which would doubtless justify a major scholarly study. Here I present some thoughts on this broad topic from the perspective of an American archaeologist with a particular background. I was trained in the 1970s at the University of Chicago under Leslie Freeman, Richard Klein and Karl Butzer, and was lucky enough to study for a time at the laboratory of François Bordes, Denise de Sonneville-Bordes and their associates at the Université de Bordeaux I. In my doctoral and subsequent research I have been principally concerned with the period of the Middle-Upper Paleolithic transition in western Europe, especially France. These experiences have inevitably influenced my perceptions and knowledge of the encounter between American and Continental (particularly French) Paleolithic archaeologists.

The history of this encounter is in fact a relatively long one, extending back before the First World War. In 1913 the American George Grant MacCurdy visited the Dordogne, asking Denis Peyrony's permission to excavate a Paleolithic site; with some misgivings, Peyrony allowed him to excavate for a season at the Middle and Upper Paleolithic site of La Combe, on

which he duly published a report (MacCurdy 1914) in *American Anthropologist*. MacCurdy was later to excavate at the Abri des Merveilles in the 1920s (MacCurdy 1931), but his brief publications on his work in France seem to have had little influence on either side of the Atlantic.

A brief visit with greater demonstrable effect on the practice of archaeology was that of the young American archaeologist Nels Nelson to Spain in 1913. In this case, however, the effect in question was of methodology in Europe on that in America. Nelson excavated with Obermaier and Breuil at El Castillo, and apparently returned much impressed by their concern with archaeological stratigraphy at the site, and with the notable changes in artifact form over time they could demonstrate. Shortly afterwards, he began to monitor changes in artifact form and decoration within stratigraphic sequences in the U.S. Southwest, and American archaeologists finally came to pay close attention to stratigraphy (Willey and Sabloff 1993).

However, long-term, systematic work by a U.S. archaeologist in the European Paleolithic did not occur until after the Second World War. Hallam

Movius, who had long had Old World interests, worked first at the Upper Paleolithic site of La Colombière in the 1950s (Movius and Judson 1956), and then conducted his famous excavation of the Abri Pataud between 1958 and 1964 (Movius, ed., 1975). Movius was the first U.S. archaeologist to carry out and publish what were clearly important Paleolithic excavations in Europe, and the first to train American doctoral students (e.g., James Sackett and Harvey Bricker) who would themselves work for many years in French Paleolithic research. In contrast to many of his successors, though, he worked largely within the framework of conventional French prehistory. Like François Bordes and other leading French prehistorians, Movius was concerned to improve the stratigraphic resolution of Paleolithic excavations in order to excavate minimal, intact depositional and occupational units; to study stone tools systematically to maximize their information content; to utilize radiocarbon dating where possible; and to bring geology and other natural sciences to bear to reconstruct past climate and environments and correlate the sequences of different sites. Bricker (this volume) has pointed out the innovative nature of the lithic attribute-analysis work by Movius and his students, but Movius was not attempting to push Paleolithic research down a fundamentally different path than that followed by its European practicioners.

But when the "trickle" of Movius and his students was followed in the 1960s and 1970s by a "flood" of American archaeologists and their students, such a reorientation of Paleolithic research was indeed advocated by more than a few of them. Putting this "flood" into historical context requires consideration of several points. First, the influx was due in part to large-scale social and economic developments in the U.S. In the 1960s, widespread prosperity, the increasing demand for an educated workforce, and the postwar "Baby Boom" created unprecedented growth in the American higher education system. Established departments of anthropology grew, new departments were founded, and there were unprecedented numbers of anthropology students (and in time, research-active faculty), some of whom became interested in formerly obscure specialist fields like the Paleolithic. Additionally, the advent of economical travel by jet aircraft made excavation and research trips to Europe more feasible for professors and students alike.

Secondly, the growth of interest in the Old World Paleolithic by Americans coincided with some dramatic developments within American anthropology and, especially, archaeology. There was first the development of American-style paleoanthropology in the 1950s and 1960s by F. Clark Howell and other workers (e.g., Howell and Clark, eds., 1966). For Howell, paleoanthropology was the interdisciplinary study of human biobehavioral evolution, centered on the synthesis of skeletal and archaeological evidence of past human adaptations with paleoenvironmental and dating information. After working in Africa, Howell applied a paleoanthropological approach to the European Lower Paleolithic in his work at Ambrona and Torralba in Spain (1960-63) (e.g., Howell 1966). The idea that research into the Pleistocene human past must synthesize the work of physical anthropology and archaeology, two subfields of traditional "four-field" American anthropology, has continued to inform most Paleolithic research by U.S. workers.

Thirdly, the wave of Americans entering European Paleolithic studies also coincided with the advent of the "New Archaeology." This movement, also known as processual archaeology, was born in the context of four-field anthropology, as archaeologists came to argue that their subfield was not a poor stepchild, but one that could help answer major questions about the nature and operation of culture - and especially about how culture changed (and evolved?) over great expanses of time. Indeed, the Old World Paleolithic came to have a special interest to some processualists. If one was interested in issues of cultural adaptation and evolution on a time scale of the Pleistocene ice ages, or in the cultural behavior of pre-anatomically modern humans, one was forced by the relatively shallow archaeological record of the Americas to look beyond one's own shores.

Several characteristics of the New Archaeology fairly guaranteed that when its practicioners encountered their European counterparts, misunderstandings and disagreements would result. One was its very conception of archaeology as an integral part of four-field anthropology. In Europe, Paleolithic prehistory was usually seen as a discipline with a historical emphasis, distinct from anthropology (a term that on the Continent generally referred to what Americans called physical anthropology) or ethnology (the counterpart of American cultural anthropology). In American anthropology there was a long tradition of close and mutually beneficial collaboration between archaeologists and cultural anthropologists in the Southwest and elsewhere that had no close counterpart among Paleolithic prehistorians. Though the latter group certainly used ethnographic analogy sometimes, the lack of cultural continuity between any ethnographically known modern peoples and those of the remote European past made most workers very cautious about the usefulness of the ethnographic record for understanding the Paleolithic.

There was also the view of New Archaeologists that archaeology was properly a social science. As such, it should test hypotheses about the operation of cultural systems in the past. Such hypothesis testing would require appropriate sampling and statistical analysis of data, for which computers were providentially becoming available at the time. Culture was seen as a systemic whole, and it was believed that systematic relationships between cultural behavior and its archaeological residues were known, or at least would soon be charted. In this view, past human adaptations, and not the industries or "cultures" delineated by European prehistorians (e.g., Aurignacian and Magdalenian) were the object of proper interest. In contrast, most Continental prehistorians practiced what Sackett (1991) has called "straight archaeology, French style." These straight archaeologists generally concentrated on space-time systematics, tending to be both cautious and ad-hoc in their suggestions about the human behavior that gave rise to patterning in the archaeological record. Despite their usual orientation to the sciences of Quaternary geology and paleontology, they were dubious that ancient human behavior could be scientifically retrieved in detail from the archaeological record. It is worth noting that other social sciences, such as sociology and political science, tend as well to be less quantitative and self-consciously "scientific" in Europe than in the U.S.

The New Archaeology in its early years was characterized by a high degree of confidence – many would say hubris – that many aspects of past cultural systems could be reconstructed, despite the incomplete nature of the archaeological record, if correct scientific methodology were used. European prehistorians often saw such confidence as naïve, based on a lack of familiarity with the complexities and limitations of the deep Paleolithic record. American archaeologists were seen as too trusting in the possibilities of ethnographic analogy, in idealized notions of scientific method, and in computers and statistics (cf. Bordes, Rigaud and Sonneville Bordes 1972).

When the encounter came in the 1960s and early 1970s between European prehistorians and growing numbers of American processual archaeologists, it is

thus unsurprising that important disagreements ensued. The most memorable, now indeed a legendary confrontation, was between François Bordes and Lewis Binford over the interpretation of Mousterian facies variability (and recounted from the latter's perspective in Binford 1972). There were others, however. In an area of special interest to me, Lynch (1966) examined the case of Chatelperronian industry, and found the characterizations of it in the French archaeological literature wanting. He argued that once the cases of artifact collections mixed by geological forces or excavators were set aside, the remaining evidence rendered the very existence of this industry a dubious proposition. This provoked a sharp reaction in Bordeaux, communicated to me some years later, to the effect that Lynch was working without a firsthand familiarity with the sites, collections, or typology involved, and was in no position to draw conclusions on the viability of the Chatelperronian. Lynch did point out the questionable integrity of a number of sites traditionally used to define the Chatelperronian, but as luck would have it, data from a number of excavations that began to become available around the time of his publication gradually showed that he was wrong about the nonexistence of the Chatelperronian (Harrold 2000).

Disagreements have certainly continued. Differences between Americans and Europeans persist in the disciplinary and institutional contexts in which Paleolithic archaeology is practiced, the professional formation and career trajectories of archaeologists, and the vocabulary they use: what Americans call the Magdalenian tradition or culture-stratigraphic unit, their French counterparts may call a culture or even a "civilization." Such real differences encourage the perception that there are deep, even paradigmatic differences in the viewpoints of American and European Paleolithic specialists (e.g., see Clark, 1997a and this volume, and Straus, this volume). My sense is that, two generations after the Bordes-Binford confrontation, the relationship has become more complex and nuanced, and, for the most part, intellectually productive.

One aspect of the complexity of this relationship can be seen if we take the activities comprised under the term "Paleolithic research" and parse them along the lines traditionally suggested by American college textbooks in introductory archaeology. These commonly suggest that archaeological research attempts to accomplish three tasks, arranged in order of ascending abstraction: (1) culture history or time-space systematics; (2) reconstruction of past cultural systems; (3) inference of long-term cultural process (e.g., cultural "evolution"). As research questions move from the concrete to the more abstract, I think there tends to be less unanimity between Americans and Europeans on the most important activities and questions to pursue , and how to do so. At the level of time-space systematics, both Europeans and Americans tend to approach stratigraphy, chronology and methods of paleoenvironmental reconstruction in much the same way, and to readily borrow techniques and ideas from each other. One sees little difference between the groups in how sites are excavated and data of various classes are gathered.

At the level of cultural reconstruction, there is still substantial agreement on the usefulness (and the uses to be made) of techniques for inferring past areas and sequences of hominid activities, like zooarchaeology or lithic *chaîne opératoire* studies. At the level of cultural process, however, we see more notable differences in fundamental approaches and questions. Research questions for instance, are likelier to be posed by Americans than Europeans in terms of explicit hypothesis-testing, and in the language of anthropological theory informed by hunter-gatherer ethnology and ecology.

Yet even at the level of questions of long-term cultural and biological process in the Paleolithic, we do not see a simple dichotomy of approaches between Europeans and Americans. Forty years of interaction, argument, cooperative research, and accommodation have led to a complex intellectual landscape of methodological and theoretical approaches and scholarly conclusions influenced, but not determined, by nationality. There are of course many examples of successful, long-term excavations and other research collaborations between Europeans and Americans – see, for example Dibble and Debenath (1991), Simek and Rigaud, González Echegaray and Freeman (González Echegaray 2000; González Echegaray and Freeman 1998), or Straus and González Morales (2001; González Morales & Straus 2000). Sometimes, the collaborators acknowledge considerable theoretical differences, and even divergence in the research questions to be pursued with common methodology in a collaborative excavation. In other cases, the mutual influence on each collaborator's theoretical perspective is strong.

An illustration of the theoretical complexity of this landscape is afforded by the question of the fate of the Neanderthals and the related issue of the nature and significance of the Middle-Upper Paleolithic

transition in Europe. Here there are not only two models attempting to delineate what happened, and how and why, in mid-Last Glacial Europe, and no popular model has exclusively American or European support (Harrold 2000). The considerable spectrum of views on these issues can be reduced to three broad models without doing too much violence to the views of individual authors. The "acculturation and replacement" model sees the European Neanderthals as having become extinct (whether with or without interbreeding with incoming modern human populations), though acculturation from contact with moderns is invoked to explain so-called transitional industries such as the Chatelperronian, and Neanderthal archaeological association with the latter industry. Most forcefully advocated by Klein (2000) and Mellars (e.g. 1998), it has received support from a variety of workers, including both Americans (Howell 1994) and Europeans (Hublin et al. 1995, 1996; Maroto, Soler, and Fullola 1996). It might be noted parenthetically that the proposition of a dichotomous American-European paradigm clash is further complicated by the presence of British (e.g., Mellars, Gamble) and Canadian (e.g., White, Rolland) participants in the discussion.

A "continuity" or "multiregional" model is indeed most forcefully advocated by two American prehistorians (e.g., Clark 1997b, 1999; Straus 1996, 1997), and explicitly linked by them to opposition to a European "normative" paradigm. In this view, the modern/Neanderthal and Middle/Upper Paleolithic distinctions drawn by replacement advocates are overdrawn at best, and at worst, mere reifications of categories constructed in the nineteenth century. In their view, modern humans and the Upper Paleolithic emerged gradually from a complex, long-term mosaic process of biological and cultural evolution involving independent invention as well as diffusion, natural selection as well as gene flow. Here, it can be argued, is an American paradigm based on New World conceptions of science and four-field anthropology. As noted, though, a number of advocates of the replacement model are Americans, despite its putatively normative and European characteristics. At the same time, the views of Clark and Straus receive some support among Europeans, for example in the suggestion of Cabrera Valdes and Bernaldo de Quiros (1990) that the origins of the western European Aurignacian are to be found in the regional Mousterian, or that of Roebroeks and Corbey (2001) on the arbitrariness of the boundary between Middle and Upper Paleolithic.

Yet another model accepts some basic elements of replacement (of Neanderthals by moderns and of the Middle by the Upper Paleolithic). However, it denies acculturation; in a critical review of dating and other evidence, it rejects the temporal overlap between the Mousterian and the Chatelperronian (the Early Upper Paleolithic industry apparently associated with Neanderthals). Instead, it posits that the Chatelperronian represented an autochthonous development of an Upper Paleolithic by Neanderthals which antedated the Aurignacian, seen as the manifestation of modern peoples' Upper Paleolithic cultures. Like the continuity model, it denies a cognitive "great divide" between Neanderthals and moderns, as is shown, it is argued, by the apparently late survival of the Neanderthals south of the Ebro River in Iberia and perhaps elsewhere as well. This "Ebro frontier" model thus has important points of both agreement and disagreement with the two other models. While it is advanced by European workers (e.g., d'Errico et al. 1998; Zilhao and d'Errico 1999), it has been critiqued by both American and European authors on various grounds (e.g., comments in d'Errico et al. 1998 and Mellars et al. 1999; Harrold and Otte 2001).

In sum, an examination of one of the issues of the day in Paleolithic prehistory finds workers from Europe and the U.S. taking varying positions in a way which cannot be understood only in terms of a clash between New World and Old World paradigms. As noted above, there are surely some important transatlantic differences in how prehistory is performed and written. Additionally, I have the impression- not quantitatively tested- that Continental prehistorians tend to be less ready than their New World counterparts to stake a definite position on controversial issues such as the fate of the Neanderthals. Montes, Utrilla, and Hedges, for instance (2001), strike a common note when they express the concern that we do not have data of sufficient quality and quantity to satisfactorily test any of the contending models discussed above. Although this could be interpreted as evidence of a European empiricist approach which relies on the accumulation of data until "self-evident" patterns appear, it is not only Europeans who stress the shortcomings of the relevant database (e.g., Klein 2000). Furthermore, as we have seen, numerous Continental workers have not felt impeded by the state of the database from expressing definite views.

I believe that, on balance, "transatlantic prehistory" has been a positive development in the quest to understand the distant human past. American archaeologists brought with them some intellectual assets, such as a concern for explicit formulation and testing of hypotheses, and the linkage of prehistory to relevant data and theory in hunter-gatherer ethnology, human ecology, and evolutionary biology, that have enriched the study of the European Paleolithic. In turn, American anthropological archaeology has benefited from its exposure to the deep and complex Paleolithic archaeological record of Europe, the sophisticated methods developed by European prehistorians, and the impressive body of knowledge accumulated by them. I anticipate that as both American and European archaeologists increasingly work with colleagues in the former Soviet bloc, China, and elsewhere, such intellectual cross-fertilization will continue to yield benefits.

College of Natural and Social Sciences
Copeland Hall 101
University of Nebraska at Kearney
Kearney, NE 68849, U.S.A.
harroldfb@unk.edu

BIBLIOGRAPHY

BINFORD, L., 1972, *An Archaeological Perspective*. New York: Academic Press.

BORDES, F., RIGAUD, J.-P., and SONNEVILLE-BORDES, D. DE, 1972, Des buts, problèmes et limites de l'archéologie Paléolithique. *Quaternaria* 16, p. 15-34.

CABRERA VALDES, V., AND BERNALDO DE QUIROS, F., 1990, Données sur la Transition entre le Paléolithique Moyen et le Paléolithque Supérieur dans la Région Cantabrique: Révision Criticale. In *Paléolithique Moyen Récent et Paléolithique Supérieur en Europe*, edited by C. Farizy. Nemours: Mémoires du Musée de Préhistoire d'Ile de France, No. 3, p. 185-188.

CLARK, G., 1997a, Through a glass darkly: Conceptual issues in modern human origins research. In *Conceptual Issues in Modern Human Origins Research*, edited by G.A. Clark, and C.M. Willermet, pp. 60-76. Hawthorne, NY: Aldine de Gruyter.

CLARK, G., 1997b. The Middle-Upper Paleolithic transition in Europe: An American perspective. *Norwegian Archaeological Review* 30, p.25-53.

CLARK, G., 1999, Highly Visible, Curiously Intangible. *Science* 283:2029-2032.

DIBBLE, H., and A. DEBENATH, 1991, Paradigmatic differences in a collaborative research project. In *Perspectives on the Past: Theoretical Biases in Mediterranean Hunter-Gatherer Research*, edited by G. Clark. Philadelphia: University of Pennsylvania Press, p. 217-226.

D'ERRICO, F., J. ZILHAO, M. JULIEN, D. BAFFIER, and J. PELEGRIN, 1998, Neandertal Acculturation in Western Europe? A Critical Review of the Evidence and Its Interpretation. *Current Anthropology* 39:S1-S44.

GONZALEZ ECHEGARAY, J., 2000, L.G. Freeman and Spanish Prehistory. *Journal of Anthropological Research* 56, p. 11-16.

GONZALEZ ECHEGARAY, J., and L.G. FREEMAN, 1998, *Le Paléolithique Inférieur et Moyen en Espagne*. Grenoble: Jérôme Millon.

GONZÁLEZ MORALES, M. and L.G. STRAUS, 2000, La Cueva del Mirón (Ramales de la Victoria, Cantabria): Excavaciones 1996-1999. Trabajos de Prehistoria 57, n.°1, pp. 121-133.

HARROLD, F., 2000, The Chatelperronian in Historical Context. *Journal of Anthropological Research* 56, p. 59-76.

HARROLD, F and M. OTTE, 2001, Time, space, and cultural process in the European Middle-Upper Paleolithic Transition. In *Questioning the Answers: Re-Solving Fundamental Problems of the Early Upper Paleolithic*, edited by M. Hays and P. Thacker, Oxford: BAR, p.3-11.

HOWELL, F., 1966, Observations on the earlier phases of the European Lower Paleolithic. *American Anthropologist* 68 (2/2), p. 88-201.

HOWELL, F., 1994, A Chronostratigraphic and Taxonomic Framework of the Origins of Modern Humans. In *Origins of Anatomically Modern Humans*, edited by M. Nitecki and D. Nitecki. New York: Plenum Press, p. 253-319.

HOWELL, F., and J.D. CLARK, Editors, 1966, *Recent Studies in Paleoanthropology*. Special issue of *American Anthropologist* 68, No. 2, Part 2.

HUBLIN, J.-J., C. BARROSO RUIZ, P. MEDINA LARA, M. FONTUGNE, and J.-L. REYSS, 1995, Le Gisement Moustérien de Zafarraya (Andalousie, Espagne): Datation et Implications sur le Processus de Peuplement Paléolithique de l' Europe Occidentale, *Comptes-Rendus de l'Academie des Science de Paris*, Série IIa, 321, P. 931-937.

HUBLIN, J.-J., F. SPOOR, M. BRAUN, F. ZONNEVELD, and S. CONDEMI, 1996, A Late Neanderthal Associated with Upper Palaeolithic Artifacts. *Nature* 381, P. 224-226.

KLEIN, R., 2000, Archaeology and the Evolution of Human Behavior. *Evolutionary Anthropology* 9, p. 167-198.

LYNCH, T., 1966, The 'Lower Perigordian' in French Archaeology, *Proceedings of the Prehistoric Society* 32, p. 156-198.

MACCURDY, G., 1914, La Combe, A Palaeolithic Cave in the Dordogne. *American Anthropologist* 16, p. 157-184.

MACCURDY, G., 1931, The Abri des Merveilles at Castel-Merle near Sergeac (Dordogne). *Bulletin of the American School of Prehistoric Research* 32, p. 12-23.

MAROTO, J., N. SOLER, AND FULLOLA, 1996, Cultural change between the Middle and Upper Paleolithic in Catalonia. In *The Last Neandertals, The First Anatomically Modern Humans: A Tale About the Human Diversity. Cultural Change and Human Evolution: The Crisis at 40 KA BP*, edited by E. Carbonell, and M. Vaquero. Tarragona: Universitat Rovira i Virgili., p. 219-250.

MELLARS, P., 1998, The Fate of the Neanderthals, *Nature* 395, p.539-540.

MELLARS, P., M. OTTE, L. STRAUS, J. ZILHAO, and F. D'ERRICO, 1999, CA Forum on Theory in Archaeology: The Neanderthal Problem, Continued. *Current Anthropology* 40, p. 341-364.

MONTES, L., P. UTRILLA, AND R. HEDGES, 2001, Le passage Paléolithique moyen-Paléolithique supérieur dans la Vallée de l'Ebre (Espagne). Datations radiométriques des grottes de Peña Miel et Gabasa. In *Les Premiers Hommes Modernes de la Péninsule Ibérique*, edited by J. Zilhão, T. Aubry, and A. Carvalho. Lisbon: Instituto Português de Arqueologia, p. 87-102.

MOVIUS, H., editor, 1975, *Excavation of the Abri Pataud, Les Eyzies (Dordogne)*. Cambridge, MA: Peabody Museum of Archaeology and Ethnology.

MOVIUS, H., and S. JUDSON, 1956, *The Rock-Shelter of La Colombière: Archaeological and Geological Investigations of an Upper Périgordian Site near Poncin (Ain)*. Cambridge, MA: Peabody Museum of Archaeology and Ethnology.

ROEBROEKS, W., and CORBEY, R., 2001, Biases and double standards in paleoanthropology. In *Studying Human Origins: Disciplinary History and Epistemology*, edited by R. Corbey and W. Roebroeks. Amsterdam: Amsterdam University Press, p. 67-76.

SACKETT, J., 1991, Straight Archaeology, French Style: The Phylogenetic Paradigm in Historic Perspective. Pp. 109-139 in Perspectives on the

Past: Theoretical Biases in Mediterranean Hunter-Gatherer Research (ed. by G.A. Clark). Philadelphia: University of Pennsylvania Press.

STRAUS, L., 1996, Continuity or Rupture; Convergence or Invasion; Adaptation or Catastrophe; Mosaic or Monolith: Views on the Middle to Upper Paleolithic Transition in Iberia. In *The Last Neandertals, The First Anatomically Modern Humans: A Tale About the Human Diversity. Cultural Change and Human Evolution: The Crisis at 40 KA BP*, edited by E. Carbonell, and M. Vaquero. Tarragona: Universitat Rovira i Virgili., p. 203-218.

STRAUS, L., 1997, The Iberian situation between 40,000 and 30,000 B.P. in light of European models of migration and convergence. In *Conceptual Issues in Modern Human Origins Research*, edited by G. Clark & C. Willermet. New York: Aldine de Gruyter, p.235-252.

STRAUS, L., and M. GONZÁLEZ MORALES, 2001, The Upper Paleolithic in El Mirón Cave (Ramales, Cantabria, Spain). *Le Paléolithique supérieur européen. Bilan quinquennal 1996-2002.* ERAUL, p. 135-139.

WILLEY, G., and J. SABLOFF, 1993, *A History of American Archaeology*, Third Edition. San Francisco: Freeman.

ZILHAO, J., AND F. D'ERRICO, 1999, The Chronology and Taphonomy of the Earliest Aurignacian and Its Implication for the Understanding of Neandertal Extinction, *Journal of World Prehistory* 13, p. 1-68

AMERICAN AND EUROPEAN ARCHAEOLOGY OF THE PALAEOLITHIC: HOW TO MAKE USE OF DIVERGENT INTERPRETATIONS?

Janusz K. KOZLOWSKI

Résumé: La différence essentielle entre l'archéologie européenne et américaine est marquée par l'opposition du paradigme culturel-historique en Europe à un modèle qui identifie l'archéologie avec l'anthropologie en Amérique. Ces deux approches sont néanmoins complémentaires: au niveau synchronique la perspective anthropologique est nécessaire, par contre l'approche diachronique nécessite une perspective historique. En effet l'archéologie européenne a connu des approches anthropologiques (par exemple, dans le cas de travaux d'A.Leroi-Gourhan) et plusieurs chercheurs américains ont étudié les temps préhistoriques dans une perspective historique (A.Close, A.Marks, A.Montet-White, H.Movius, F.Wendorf). Le point crucial dans les controverses entre la préhistoire américaine et européenne émerge de la discussion entre F.Bordes et L.Binford autour de l' interprétation de la variabilité des entités taxonomiques. L'identification de ces entités avec les groupes ethniques a été critiqué par les chercheurs américains, aussi bien que l'interprétation des ressemblances entre ces entités dans l'espace comme l'effet de migrations. Cette position a conduit certains chercheurs américains à négliger les migrations dans les temps préhistoriques en opposition aux migrations des peuples historiques.

Abstract: The essential difference between European and American Archaeology consists in the opposition of the European cultural-historical paradigm and the American model which equates archaeology with anthropology. I believe that the two approaches are complementary: on the horizontal, synchronous level an interpretation of facts and records from anthropological perspective is indispensable, whereas the diachronic approach requires a historical perspective. It certainly cannot be claimed that European archaeologists do not use anthropological models (the best example are the anthropological models proposed by A.Leroi-Gourhan) or that none of American researchers have ever used the historical perspective (A. Close, A. Marks, A. Montet-White, H. Movius, F. Wendorf et al. have successfully done so). The point at issue in the controversy between European and American archaeology – stemming from the dispute between Bordes and Binford – has often been narrowed down to interpretation of inter-site variability, namely: European researchers are popularly though to interpret this variability as an expression of ethnic (or ethnographic) differences, while American archaeologists are generally believed to explain inter-site variability as a manifestation of functional differences. In reality, advance in archaeological research has shown that the causes of inter-site variability must have been much more complex and no one-sided interpretation can fully account for the diversity of archaeological facts. Similarly, the explanation whereby the similarities between some taxonomic units are interpreted as the effect of migrations – an interpretation strongly criticized by American archaeologists – cannot be totally disregarded. Were we to restrict the drive for migration to only historical times and peoples then Man would have never moved out of the boundaries of Africa. If we concede the existence of, and respect the ability of Man's mind to discover and create spontaneously we should equally concede the existence of Man's inherent curiosity, the drive to move on and "find out."

SUMMARY

The essential difference between European and American archaeology consists in the opposition of the European cultural-historical paradigm and the American model which equates archaeology with anthropology. I believe that the two approaches are complementary: on the horizontal: synchronous level an interpretation of facts and records from anthropological perspective is indispensable, whereas the diachronic approach requires a historical perspective. It certainly cannot be claimed that European archaeologists do not use anthropological models (the best examples are the anthropological models proposed by A. Leroi-Gourhan) or that none of American researchers have ever used the historical perspective (A. Close, A. Marks, A. Montet-White, H. Movius, F. Wendorf and others all have successfully done so). The point at issue in the controversy between European and American archaeology – stemming from the dispute between Bordes and Binford – has often been narrowed down to interpretation of inter-site or inter-assemblage variability, namely: European researchers are popularly though to interpret this variability as an expression of ethnic (or ethnographic) differences, while American archaeologists are generally believed to explain inter-site variability as a manifestation of functional differences. In reality, advances in archaeological research have shown that the causes of inter-site variability must have been much more complex and no one-sided interpretation can fully account for the diversity of archaeological facts. Similarly, the explanation whereby the similarities between some taxonomic units are interpreted as the effect of migrations – an interpretation strongly criticized by some American archaeologists – cannot be totally disregarded. Were we to restrict the drive for migration to only historical times and peoples, then man would have never moved out of the boundaries of Africa. If we concede the existence of, and respect the ability of man's mind to discover and create spontaneously we should equally concede the existence of man's inherent curiosity, the drive to move on and "find out".

Undoubtedly, confronting European prehistory with American prehistory is difficult because in European archaeology after all much earlier than American dominant trends kept changing. The development of European prehistory begins with the 19th century evolutionism which treated artefacts as *fossiles directeurs* and human culture as developing in accordance with mechanisms that are identical with biological ones. The next stage in Europe was "cultural archaeology" based on the identification of diagnostic types that defined taxonomic units – archaeological cultures – with ethnic units. The paradigm of identification of taxonomic units with peoples still dominates in European prehistory independently of modifications brought later by Marxism with its naive faith in the determining importance of infrastructure (forces and relations of production) in relation to superstructure (ideology and politics), or by New Archaeology with its neo-positivistic faith in all-applying laws and rules of social and cultural development in prehistory. Apart from these paradigms, a lasting value of European prehistory has been its historical approach, similar to *histoire événementielle,* in F. Braudel's (1967, 1971) sense expressing – under the appearances of superficial happenings – slower rhythms and long-term trends.

Contrary to the historical approach of European prehistory the processual approach of American anthropological archaeology placed emphasis on the study of different processes within one society and between societies, stressing the interaction of a vast number of systems: environment, ecology, technology, social relations, beliefs, etc. Processual interpretation implies the discovery of regularities between particular sub-systems in the sense of Carl Hempel's "natural laws" (1949, 1965). In this way the explanation of archaeological facts acquires a deductive-nomothetic character.

In archaeological practice, explanation means the resolution of the fundamental problem of the interpretation of taxonomic units distinguished by two systems (artefact-attribute-type and type-assemblage-"culture"). In the European school, a prevalent paradigm interprets cultures as ethnic (linguistic) units – and in the past also as racial – in the understanding of physical anthropology – entities. An effective criticism of this paradigm derives from American archaeology and the processual approach attaching importance to functional and environmental determinants of both artefacts (and their frequency) and assemblages combined, subsequently, into "cultures".

The first attempt at such interpretation was undertaken by L. Binford and S. Binford (1966) who explained Mousterian units as the result of specific functions of camps, while Mousterian assemblages are the remains of such camps. F. Bordes (1953) interpreted taxonomic units, distinguished in the Mousterian on the basis of frequencies of particular tool types in assemblages, as ethnic units, whereas L. Binford proposed a functional interpretation of the differences between Mousterian facieses. The polemic between F. Bordes and L. Binford has been doubtless of fundamental importance for the criticism of the cultural paradigm in European prehistory. In the 1980s, American archaeology made further attempts at the explanation of taxonomic units of the Middle Palaeolithic. H. Dibble (1987) tried to account for the variability of morphology of side-scrapers on the facieses distinguished by F. Bordes, by the differing degree of reduction of side-scrapers. N. Rolland (1981) investigated the relation between Mousterian facieses and various types of environment. These new interpretations proposed by the archaeology of the New World had a positive influence on the critical review of the cultural paradigm of European prehistory. However, they were all really monocausal, which was their principal weakness. Now, at the beginning of the XXIst century, it seems that it is time for multivariate explanations that would integrate a number of factors. Naturally, to create multivariate explanations is complex and difficult as we are having to do with a large number of variables that vary simultaneously.

Another important field of confrontation of American and European archaeology is the problem of explanation of cultural change. In this area of study European archaeology is dominated by a migrationist paradigm: when each archaeological culture corresponds to a well-defined ethnic group, then a cultural change is interpreted as folk migration. Moreover, maps of the distribution of archaeological cultures provide in European archaeology the grounds for the identification of homeland for a given group or people, and chronological sequences within cultural distribution patterns enable to identify migration routes. This has led to the preference for diffusionist models in European archaeology.

American archaeology could not altogether avoid migrationist interpretations if only because the settling of the New World was the result of migration from Asia – if we disregard extreme hypotheses that wish to derive Palaeoindians from the European Upper Palaeolithic. Nor has American archaeology managed to do without the concept of diffusion (if at least in the question of origins of ceramics in the territory of the New World, or the explanation of the amazing cultural development in the south-western part of the USA by the diffusion of influences from advanced Mesoamerican civilizations). Nonetheless, the prevailing tendency in American archaeology is to explain cultural change by inner developmental dynamics, transformation and adaptation to changing conditions of natural environment rather then by a change of population. This tendency has caused some American scholars (e.g., G. A. Clark, 1994) to negate outright the existence of migrations in prehistoric times, restricting them to historical times. Such an approach was the result of a different understanding of migration on the scale of prehistoric times: historical migrations were processes observable by a single generation, whereas populations shifts in prehistoric times were a much slower processes, often barely noticeable at the generational scale, as in the case of small shifts of the range of annual migrations of hunting-gathering peoples. Such shifts were not necessarily caused or enforced by demographic pressure.

Criticism originating from the circles of the American school also concerned diffusion, for example in the case of L. Binford's (1968) explanation of the farming revolution. The consequence of the criticism of diffusionist model was the rejection of the role of

migrations in the spread of farming economy in the territory of the Old World and especially in the European continent. In the same way, the diffusionist-migration model applied to the appearance of modern humans in Europe and the transition from the Middle to Upper Palaeolithic has also been criticized and replaced by multiregional evolution.

Palaeogenetic investigations have shown that an outright condemnation of the diffusionist-migrationist approach is unjustified. The most important stages in cultural changes (at the transition from the Middle to the Upper Palaeolithic, at the boundary of the Mesolithic and the Neolithic, also at the Upper and Final Palaeolithic boundary) correlate well with the influx of new genetic material substantiating migrations (Torroni et al. 1998).

The explanation of cultural change either as a change of population only, or as adaptational processes only, reveals all the weaknesses of monocausal explanation. In reality, analysis of cultural changes – especially at the key moments in prehistory such as the Middle/Upper Palaeolithic transition – indicate that these were processes with many complex causes and complicated courses, not always unidirectional (for example, the repeated appearance of the blade technique). Within the process of cultural change were superimposed processes of change and increases of population, internal evolution, new inventions appearing convergently in different territories, changes in social systems, systems of belief and communication. For all these reasons, I would see the future of archaeology in the XXIst century in terms of multivariate explanations which require us to combine the diffusionist-migrationist and evolutionist perspectives. Explanatory models become, in effect, more and more intricate. This makes us move away from the dichotomus (bimodal), simplistic concepts of the XXth century, but may also impede our grasp of general trends.

Universytet Jagiellonski
Instytut Archeologii
Golebia, 11
31-007 Krakow, POLAND
kozlowsk@argo.hist.uj.edu.pl

BIBLIOGRAPHY

BINFORD L.R., 1968. Post-Pleistocene adaptations (in) *New Perspectives in Archaeology* (ed.by S.R.Binford and L.R.Binford) pp.313-341.

BINFORD L.R., BINFORD S.R., 1966. A preliminary analysis of functional variabilityin the Mousterian of Levallois facies. *American Anthropology*, 68, 2, pp.238-295.

BORDES F., 1953. Essai de classification des industries mousteriennes. *Bulletin de la SPF*, 50, pp. 457-466.

BRAUDEL F., 1967. Civilisation materielle et capitalisme de XV-XVIII s. Paris.

CLARK G.A., 1994. Migrations as an explanatory concept in Paleolithic archaeology. *Journal of Archaeological Method and Theory*, 1, 4, pp.305-343.

DIBBLE H., 1987. The interpretation of Middle Palaeolithic scraper morphology. *American Antiquity*, 52, 1, pp.109-117.

HEMPEL C.G., 1949. The function of general laws in history (in:) *Readings in Philosphical Analysis* (ed.by H.Feigl and E.G.Sellers). New York, pp.459-471.

HEMPEL C.G., 1965. Aspects pf scientific explanation and other essays on the philosophy of science. New York.

ROLLAND N., 1981. The interpretation of Middle Palaeolithic variability. *Man*, 16, pp.15-42.

TORRONI A., BANDELT H.J., d'URBANO L., LAHERMO P., MORAL P., SELLITO D., RENGO C., FORSTER P., SAVONTAUS M.L., BONNE-TAMIT B., SCOZZARI R., 1998. MtDNA Analysis reveals a major Late Palaeolithic population expansion from Southwestern to Northeastern Europe. *American Journal of Human Genetics*, 62, pp.1137-1152.

LE RÔLE DES AMÉRICAINS DANS LA RECHERCHE DU PALÉOLITHIQUE EN EUROPE

Marcel OTTE

Résumé: La recherche fut organisée en Europe de façon plus rigoureuse sous l'influence américaine. Elle fut mieux argumentée sur le plan méthodologique. Cependant, l'influence de « modèles théoriques » fut parfois contraignante et réductrice sur le plan historique. L'apport de Hallam Movius fut certainement le plus exemplaire, par les méthodes des fouilles, d'analyse et de datation. Les modèles ethnographiques et l'approche anthropologique sont venus compléter la démarche plus strictement évolutive en Europe.

Abstract: Paleolithic research in Europe became organized more rigorously under American influence and methodologically in was better argued. However, on the historical level, the influence of "theoretical models" has sometimes been constraining and reductionist. The contribution of the late Hallum Movius was certainly the most exemplary in terms of excavation methods, analysis & dating. Ethnographic models and the anthropological approach in general have complemented the more strictly evolutionary approach normally taken in Europe.

L'influence américaine a soufflé à diverses reprises comme un vent frais sur la Préhistoire d'Europe. Il était vivifiant tant qu'il n'emportait pas tout ! Les chercheurs américains ont souvent eu tendance à remettre en cause les théories historiques dominantes et à les soumettre à l'épreuve des faits, contrôlés et démontrés.

Le point de vue extérieur dont on dispose depuis l'Amérique fournit une vision plus globale et, fatalement, plus « professionnelle », donc totalement dépourvue de fantaisie. Cette activité se veut là-bas « scientifique », comme si une phobie d'accéder au niveau humaniste poussait les chercheurs américains à se réfugier sous le parapluie commode des sciences simplement « exactes ».

De l'autre côté, nos vieilles écoles européennes furent trop solidement attachées à leur région, construisant une histoire verticale du lieu, comme s'il s'agissait d'une continuité locale. De nombreux exemples illustrent à quel point cette tendance peut être erronée, voire sinistre, lorsqu'elle prend la forme du nationalisme, très fervent, autant en France qu'en Allemagne au cours du XXᵉ siècle.

Pour un chercheur américain, la nécessité de traverser l'Atlantique à chaque fouille constitue automatiquement un « tri institutionnel » que ne subissait pas l'Européen à qui il suffisait parfois de traverser son champ cultivé ou son presbytère. Bien plus qu'un Européen, le préhistorien venu d'Amérique doit rendre compte d'importants moyens confiés par son gouvernement ou des fondations privées. Si cette différence tend à se réduire aujourd'hui par la création des Institutions européennes, elle traverse néanmoins tout le XXᵉ siècle, accentuant encore les oppositions dues par ailleurs aux conceptions différentes des sciences anthropologiques.

Par cette tendance très professionnelle (c'est-à-dire très subsidiée), un sens aigu des responsabilités, typiquement américain, fut importé en Europe, où il provoqua des aires de troubles et de malentendus, dans des milieux européens naturellement plus décontractés et plus romantiques. [Dans les années soixante, cette différence de sensibilité fut particulièrement évidente au travers du jeu d'école entretenu entre Fr. Bordes et H. Movius aux Eyzies.] Tandis que la vision américaine englobait l'Europe (Movius, 1975), l'Afrique du Nord (Howe, 1967), le Proche-Orient (Solecki, 1971) et l'Asie centrale (Movius, 1951 ; Hole & Flannery, 1967), celle des Européens eut tendance à fragmenter en autant d'histoires régionales des processus dissociés en fait par les langues, les nations, leurs régimes politiques et leurs traditions actives actuellement.

L'un des critères distinctifs entre l'Ancien et le Nouveau Monde fut cette association, si étrange aux yeux des Européens, d'audace et de rigueur apportée par les chercheurs américains. En Europe, ces deux qualités restent trop souvent dissociées, voire opposées, dans la démarche archéologique. Adolescent, je subis une forte impression au contact de H. Movius, torturé par un idéal de vérité qu'un devoir impérieux lui imposait d'atteindre, selon les voies, austères et rigides, de la « démarche scientifique », suspicieuse de la critique et en perpétuelle inquiétude. Rien n'est comparable aux intuitions fulgurantes d'André Leroi-Gourhan ou de Gordon Childe. Chez nous hélas, l'audace se marie moins avec la rigueur et nous participons le plus souvent à l'un ou à l'autre de ces états d'esprit, pour le meilleur et pour le pire.

Une troisième dimension fit toutefois souvent défaut aux chercheurs américains, celle liée à la pesanteur historique, responsable des traditions culturelles en préhistoire. Outre-Atlantique, il faudrait savoir admettre que l'histoire ne présente pas d'autre valeur qu'en soi, et ne répond à aucune loi logique simple. Ceci semble provoquer en Amérique une sorte de terreur qui fit ranger le sens historique dans une zone inexplicable, donc taboue.

Sûrement, cette idée fut acceptée en Europe de façon beaucoup plus confortable. Mais nous nous sommes trop facilement contentés de cette certitude aveuglante qui, souvent, se substitua à un effort d'explication d'un phénomène humain, fut-il des plus anodins. Ainsi, en Europe, s'est-on souvent contenté de reproduire des « faits » sans leur donner aucun sens ! Ce qui est la perversion de la démarche historique.

Cependant, le comportement humain évoluant au fil du temps, ne peut se trouver justifié par des lois à échelle courte, comme le jeu entretenu entre l'homme et son environnement, ses ressources et ses variations. En apparence, aucune explication simple ne peut rencontrer le choix évidemment arbitraire pratiqué par diverses traditions dans un environnement identique. À force d'être pénétrés par cette évidence, nous avons eu tendance en Europe à l'accepter comme une explication. Les reflets matériels livrés par la préhistoire n'expriment sans doute qu'un rapport métaphysique entretenu par tel groupe humain avec la nature. Sur cette banalité, les écoles européennes ont bâti leur discipline préhistorique, sans se soucier davantage de son fondement : les systèmes de pensée se valent, pour un même contexte, et il nous suffit d'en discerner les contours pour que la matière historique s'exprime, en quelque sorte d'elle-même. La déficience se place là, en même temps que le confort où s'installent volontiers les préhistoriens européens.

Ainsi, peut-on facilement comprendre les dérives nationalistes que ne peuvent éviter les développements progressivement suivis par une telle pensée. Aujourd'hui encore, on assiste à la célébration insipide de l'esprit « gaulois » dans une nation faite de Francs (peuples germaniques) retrouvant de curieuses racines par-delà la colonisation romaine subie pendant plus de quatre siècles.

L'exemple allemand n'est pas moins grave lorsque l'on songe à la théorie nazie fondée sur l'illusion d'une appartenance à un peuple *et* à une race (!) aux origines de l'Europe protohistorique et de la Nation au xxe siècle. En réalité, toutes les tendances nationalistes en préhistoire européenne se déplacent aux bords d'un gouffre idéologique, car la notion de « patrimoine » chez nous prend facilement le sens d'un symbole d'authenticité, de légitimité et de justification d'une action politique. De frais exemples issus du Proche-Orient ravivent quotidiennement cette récupération de la préhistoire, à laquelle très naturellement la plupart des chercheurs américains ont jusqu'ici échappé (et, derrière eux, les Britanniques).

Parmi bien d'autres, un exemple retentissant fut donné dans la reconstitution de la genèse du Solutréen. En simplifiant, on vit d'y opposer l'arbre « phylétique » des cultures régionales (c'est-à-dire de l'Aquitaine) à partir d'une hypothétique souche locale (Smith, 1966 : fig. 82) à l'évidente analogie entre les industries de Tanger et celles de l'Espagne solutréenne (Howe, 1967) (Fig. 1-2). D'un trait de plume, Denise de Sonneville-Bordes (1972 : 97 ; voir aussi 1959 : 8) balaya l'argument et fut suivie par l'Europe entière et tout rentra dans l'ordre...

La perspective volontiers ethnographique (on dit « anthropologique », aux États-Unis) suivie, telle une épidémie, par de nombreux chercheurs américains juvéniles et fascinés, accentue encore ce divorce avec l'Europe. Tout à l'encontre de la préhistoire, cette mode des « modèles » fonctionne exclusivement sur la synchronie et considère le site préhistorique comme figé dans un « moment » illusoire.

Comme si tout était transposable d'un coin à l'autre de la planète tant qu'il s'agit de populations primitives, tout y est amalgamé joyeusement, des Inuits arctiques à Pincevent sur Seine (L. Binford). En fait, l'insistance portée sur les processus de formation des sites dissimule mal le mépris accordé à leur signification historique. Là encore, un fossé profond sépare les écoles des deux rives de l'Atlantique.

Dans un pays où Claude Levi-Strauss produisit ses meilleures œuvres, l'approche anthropologique ne fut

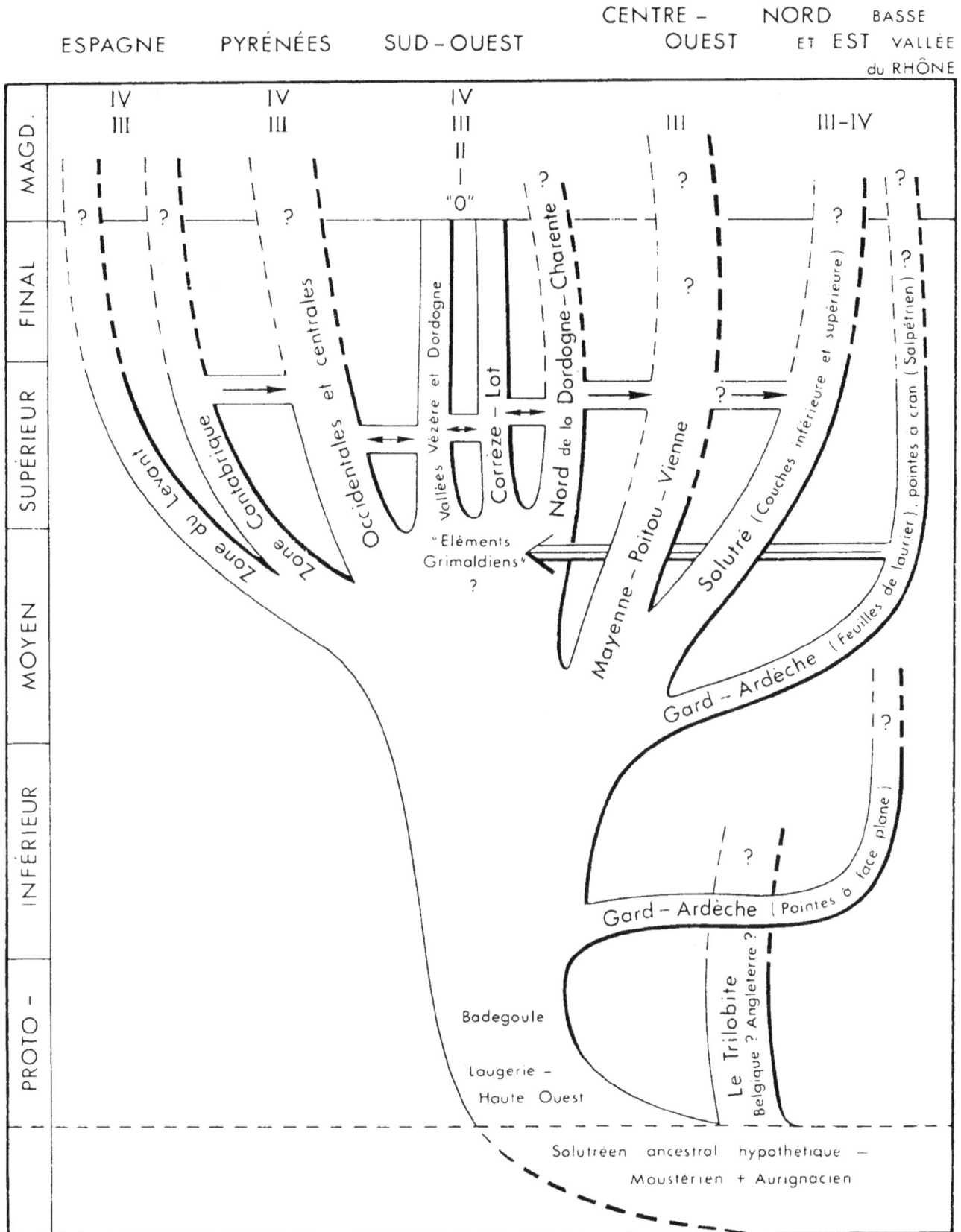

Figure 1. En Europe, la vision historique est souvent conçue comme un arbre phylétique dont les racines plongent dans le territoire national, jusqu'en plein Paléolithique (d'après Smith, 1966).

sûrement pas négligée. Toutefois, elle ne peut atteindre le fonctionnement social dans son mécanisme évolutif, ce qui, précisément, constitue l'objet de la Préhistoire, science de la durée.

Ainsi, les écoles américaines devraient continuer à provoquer les chercheurs européens, par leurs idées nouvelles et leurs perpétuelles remises en question d'un raisonnement tendant à l'inertie historique et

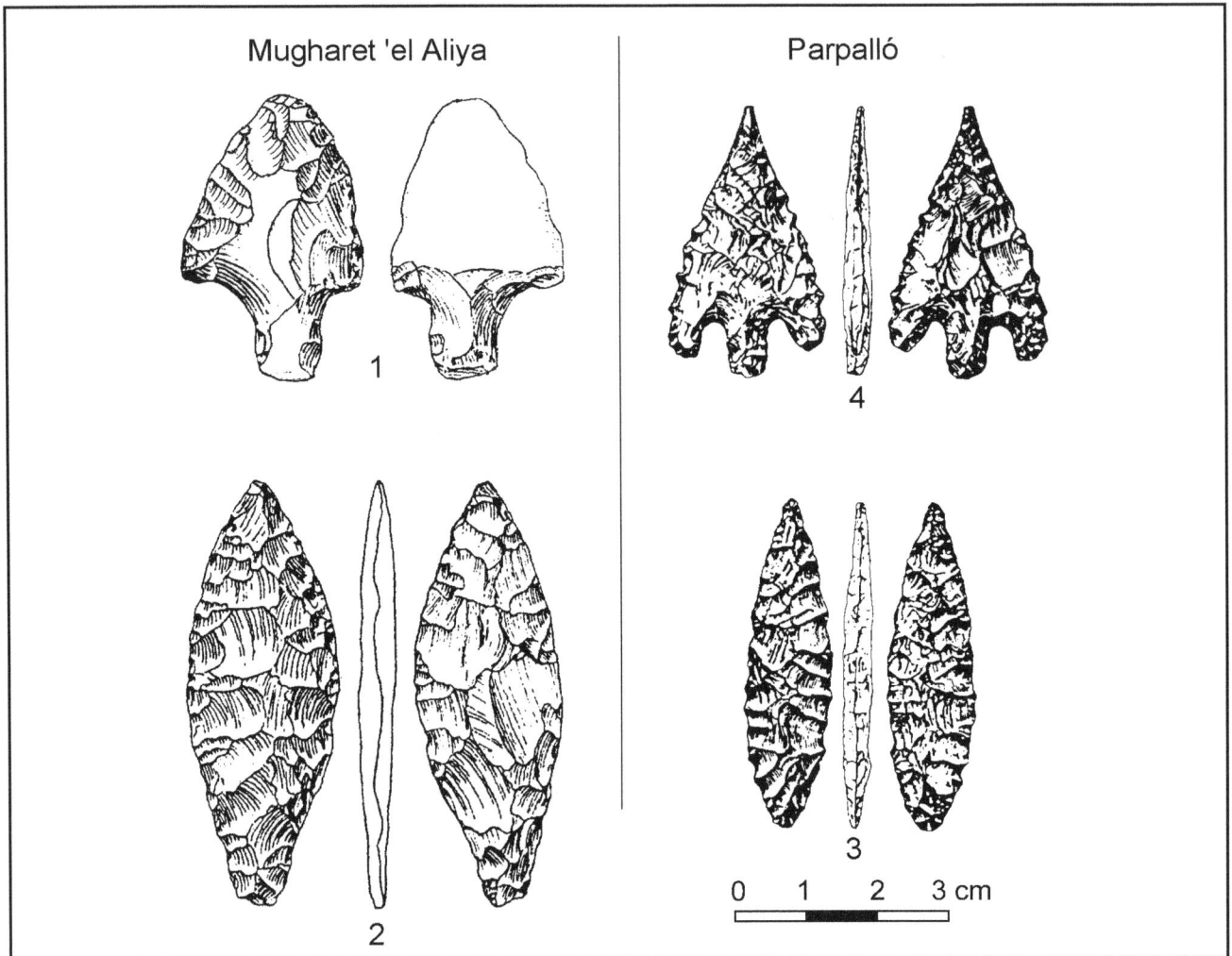

Figure 2. Bruce Howe a vainement tenté de briser ce carcan par des analogies techniques de grande envergure (dans ce cas-ci, le Maroc). Venues de trop loin, ces vues sont restées ignorées (1-2 : grotte Mugharet 'el Aliya, Tanger, Maroc, couche 6, d'après Howe, 1967 ; 3 : Parpalló, Solutréen « moyen », et 4 : Solutréen « supérieur », d'après Pericot, dans Howe, 1967).

volontiers séduit par des sirènes nationalistes auxquelles échappe spontanément l'Américain. Fondons aussi l'espoir que les écoles européennes sauront résister à des explications mécanistes trop simples, liées par exemple aux contraintes de l'environnement. Comme notre histoire européenne, la préhistoire a évolué dans un milieu flou et subtil, fait de pensée, d'art et de tradition. Aucune loi n'enferme les quêtes d'identité à chaque moment de notre évolution. En apparence, ces deux tendances se complètent et se stimulent, mais elles ne devraient jamais se confondre, afin d'y préserver toutes les richesses respectives.

Service de Préhistorie
Université de Liège
Place du XX Août, 7-A1
4000 Liège, BELGIUM
marcel.otte@ulg.ac.be

BIBLIOGRAPHY

HOLE, F.R. & FLANNERY, K.V., 1967. The Prehistory of Southwestern Iran: A preliminary report. *Proceedings of the Prehistoric Society*, XXXIII: 147-206.

HOWE, BR., 1967. The Palaeolithic of Tangier, Morocco. Excavations at Cape Ashlar, 19391947. American School of Prehistoric Research, Peabody Museum, Harvard University, Bulletin n° 22, 200 p.

MOVIUS, H.L. Jr., 1951. Teshik-Tash: A Mousterian cave site in Central Asia. *Mélanges en hommage au Professeur Hamal-Nandrin*, Bruxelles, Société Royale belge d'Anthropologie et de Préhistoire, p. 72-83.

MOVIUS H.L. Jr. (dir.), 1975. Excavation of the Abri Pataud, Les Eyzies (Dordogne). *American School of Prehistoric Research*, Bulletin 30.

SMITH, PH., 1966. Le Solutréen en France. Bordeaux, Delmas (Publications de l'Institut de Préhistoire de l'Université de Bordeaux, Mémoire n° 5), 449 p.

SOLECKI, R., 1971. *Shanidar. The First Flower People.* New York, A. Knopf.

SONNEVILLE-BORDES, D. de, 1959. Problèmes généraux du Paléolithique supérieur dans le Sud-Ouest de la France (suite). L'Anthropologie, 63 (1-2) : 1–14.

SONNEVILLE-BORDES, D. de, 1972, La Préhistoire moderne. L'âge de la pierre taillée. Périgueux, Pierre Fanlac Éditeur, 2ᵉ édition, 143 p.

YANKS (AND CANUCKS) IN THE ABBÉ BREUIL'S COURT: NOTES ON THE ROLE OF AMERICAN ARCHEOLOGISTS IN THE STUDY OF THE EUROPEAN UPPER PALEOLITHIC

Lawrence Guy STRAUS

Résumé: L'engagement des archéologues américains et canadiens dans l'étude du Paléolithique supérieur européen se divise en trois phases, introduites par un prologue et suivies par un épilogue:

Prologue. Acquisition des premières collections par des grands musées (surtout le Smithsonian) dès la fin du 19ième siècle et premières visites aux sites français et espagnols (G.G.MacCurdy, H.F.Osborn, N.C.Nelson) peu avant la Grande Guerre. Les américains prennent contact.

1. Années 20: Création de l' "American School of Prehistoric Research" par MacCurdy; visites à des sites classiques du Périgord, Pyrénées, Cantabres, Moravie, etc. et "fouilles" (plus ou moins sérieuses) par des étudiants d'universités d'élite et des collaborations (par exemple: J.T.Russell et H.Bégouën; H.Ami et D.Peyrony); grands achats par des musées américains (surtout H. Field par l'intermédiaire de Breuil); l'époque "romantique" et aventurière des dilettantes. Les américains apprennent et achètent.

2. Après la Deuxième Guerre Mondiale, H.L. Movius fait la grande fouille de l'Abri Pataud (American School et Harvard) et apporte des crédits, des idées anthropologiques, des nouvelles méthodes et plusieurs étudiants qui feraient leurs thèses de doctorat sur des industries du Paléolithique supérieur français. Les américains essaient à mettre de l'ordre.

3. Le grand débat transatlantique sur la nature et explications de la variabilité parmi les ensembles industriels paléolithiques (L. et S. Binford, Freeman contre F.Bordes et D.de Sonneville-Bordes): Fonction ou ethnicité? Culture-écologie contre histoire culturelle? L'école de Michigan et Chicago lance des fouilles et des analyses, surtout en Espagne suite des travaux de F.C.Howell et L.G.Freeman et leurs étudiants. Les américains essaient à "s'imposer".

Epilogue: Rapprochements, non seulement méthodologiques, sinon aussi philosophiques, avec une diversité de points de vue et de problèmes considérés dignes de résolution, surtout engagés dans tous les domaines depuis la subsistance à l'organisation sociale et l'idéologie préhistoriques. Collaborations authentiques et fertilisation scientifique mutuelle.

Abstract: American involvement in the study of the European Upper Paleolithic began in the late 19th century with the acquisition of artifact collections by a few East Coast museums and, in the years immediately preceding World War I, visits to sites in France and Spain by G.G.MacCurdy and H.F.Osborn. Between the world wars, MacCurdy organized the American School of Prehistoric Research, leading students mainly from elite universities in summer courses of study that included excavations of varying length (and seriousness) and visits to sites, mainly in southwest France, but also in Spain and Czechoslovakia. Other Americans and at least one important Canadian (H. Ami) made significant collections during this period, by purchase and/or excavation, in enterprises that sometimes had the **dilettante** flavor of romantic adventure. In these ways, major institutions such as the American Museum of Natural History, the Harvard Peabody Museum, the Field Museum and the Smithsonian, and also the Beloit Logan Museum, obtained large collections of Upper Paleolithic artifacts - especially from France. This upper class activity halted with the Depression and World War II. The period immediately after World War II was dominated by H.L.Movius, whose excavation of l'Abri Pataud brought a large infusion of research funds, new **anthropological** ideas, fresh excavation, dating and analytical methods, and numerous North American graduate students who went on to do important Ph.D. dissertations on French Upper Paleolithic materials. In concert with significant theoretical and methodological developments pioneered by F.Bordes and A.Leroi-Gourhan, the next phase of American involvement was launched with the seminal debate over the significance of inter-assemblage variability in both the Middle and Upper Paleolithic: the direct Binfordian challenge to the until-then unchallenged and monolithic culture-historic or phylogenetic "explanation" imposed by Breuil and his successors. Relatively abundant funding (NSF and various private foundations) and the excitement of this debate, plus the spread of paleoanthropological education westward in the U.S., generated much larger numbers of students (first at the Universities of Michigan and Chicago and soon thereafter in the West) who went on to do dissertations on various European Upper Paleolithic subjects and, in some cases, to continue doing analyses and even their own excavations in association with European colleagues - and not only in the favorite "haunts" of American archeologists between the two wars (Périgord and Pyrenees), but also in Spain, Italy, Central and Eastern Europe. Subsequent diversification of interests and viewpoints - despite differences in training respectively within anthropology or within history or geology - has brought increasing convergence between American and European approaches to Upper Paleolithic prehistory, not only in recovery and interdisciplinary analytical methods, but also in the recognition of multi-layered explanations of the record: functional, social, ethnic and ideological.

INTRODUCTION

The history of significant American involvement in the study of the European Upper Paleolithic (as well as of the Mesolithic and rest of the Paleolithic) spans most of the 20th century, beginning after World War I and accelerating markedly after World War II. This history has gone through three major phases in terms of the kind of the work conducted by Americans in Europe and with regard to the nature of their intellectual interactions with European specialists. The Euro-American relationship in Paleolithic research has been a complex one, beginning with theoretical dependence of the Americans on the Europeans and, sometimes, financial dependence of the Europeans on the Americans, followed by a period during which many of the "new ideas" were coming from the Americans and with frequent continuation of the situation of economic inequality, and finally the present period which is generally characterized by both intellectual and financial parity. The prologue to our tale involves the first purchases of Paleolithic artifacts by East Coast museums in the latter third of the 19th century without direct engagement by Americans in Europe until a few visits made to sites on the eve of the First World War.

The first (inter-war) phase involved a few Americans conducting (usually comparatively minor) excavations, mainly at French sites under the guidance of major European prehistorians of the period and fully within the culture-historical paradigm of the age. The aim of these excavations (or collecting trips) seems to have been particularly oriented toward the acquisition of lithic and osseous artifacts "typical" of the main periods **à la** de Mortillet/Breuil for American museums, as well as the training of students. This "pioneering" phase was characterized by the work of Henri-Marc Ami of the National Museum of Canada, George Collie and Alonzo Pond of the Beloit College Logan Museum, George Grant MacCurdy of Yale University and in association with the Smithsonian Institution and American School of Prehistoric Research (ASPR), Ruth O. Sawtell of Radcliffe College and the Harvard Peabody Museum, together with Ida Treat(formerly of Western Reserve University) and Treat's husband, Paul Valliant-Couturier, and J. Townsend Russell of the Smithsonian U.S. National Museum (now the National

Museum of Natural History). It was during this period that other museums (e.g., American Museum of Natural History in New York, Peabody Museums of Harvard and Yale University, Field Museum in Chicago, University of Pennsylvania Museum) were also actively acquiring artifacts "representative" of the various Stone Age periods, especially from France. American institutions often bought collections from French prehistorians in the era before Pétain's French National Antiquities Law, although exchanges for American artifacts were also made (e.g., Bahn & Cole 1986; White 1992; Petraglia & Potts n.d.).

The second phase (roughly from the late 1940s through the mid-1960s) was dominated by the work and influence of Hallam Movius of Harvard and the ASPR. Movius first dug at La Colombière rockshelter and then directed the major, methodologically seminal excavation of l'Abri Pataud in Les Eyzies - the town which is the so-called "capital of prehistory". He and his students (Philip Smith, James Sackett, Harvey Bricker, Berle Clay, Nicholas David and Alison Brooks) brought new methods (e.g., radiocarbon dating, artifact attribute analysis) and a new anthropological and ecological perspective to the study of the classic Upper Paleolithic of Aquitaine and other regions of France, but without fundamentally challenging the nature of the prehistoric enterprise as then led by Denise de Sonneville-Bordes and François Bordes at the Université de Bordeaux, despite Movius' (1953) expressed skepticism about the phylogenetic approach to the study of Stone Age techno-complexes.

The third phase (approximately from the mid-late 1960s through the 1990s) saw a larger number of Americans from many universities all over the U.S. (not only elite East Coast institutions) doing dissertations on a wide variety of Upper Paleolithic problems in many European countries (not only France). The initial enthusiasm for involvement in the European record came from the stimulating debate between Bordes (on the culture-historical/ ethnicity side) and Lewis and Sally Binford (for the processualist/functionalist perspective) over the significance of variability among Mousterian artifact assemblages, which was extended into the domain of the Upper Paleolithic principally by Sally Binford (1972). This debate sparked a wave of interest in **interpretation**, as opposed to description and classification as ultimate goals. While the interpretations tended initially to concentrate on artifact function, subsistence and other "bread-and-butter" issues, other, less tangible aspects of terminal Pleistocene human adaptations (social organization, artistic activity, ideology, human agency - including gender role differences) were also always on the table, and have increasingly become the "main course" of numerous "post-processual" researchers based in America. The new philosophical diversity and spirit of compromise represent the epilogue to this tale.

It has been in this third phase of American involvement in the study of the Upper Paleolithic that a fundamental difference between many American and many European researchers came clearly into focus, although some degree of **rapprochement** has become evident in recent years. This difference has to do with operative definitions of "culture": American archeologists, generally educated within an anthropological milieu, acknowledge multiple meanings of this key concept, following Kroeber and Kluckhohn. However, most American archeologists working in Europe from the late 1960s on, have seen the advantage of privileging Leslie White's (1959) definition of culture as "the extrasomatic means of behavior", stressing its more practical and hence archeologically visible, accessible aspects. This is also a generalizing view of the concept of culture which stands in sharp contrast to the partitive definition by which cultures (plural) are distinct ethnically identified groups. Cultures in this sense are bounded collections of socially learned and shared norms, beliefs and traditions. In an archeological sense, assemblages of material remains are thought to be different as the consequence of their reflecting such different ways or styles of making things, hence making prehistoric ethnic groups observable through the archeological record. This is the (usually unstated, but widely assumed) underlying basis of culture-historical description and classification in prehistory. The presumed study of prehistoric cultures or "peoples" through the documentation and analysis of differences and similarities among artifacts has been the credo of European prehistoric archeologists (generally educated within history or natural sciences, but not anthropology) since the decline of 19th century social evolutionism. In many cases, even American "post-processualist" archeologists have a more multifaceted view of the concept of culture than

some European colleagues, who are still enamored of the use of undifferentiated trait lists as putative indicators of prehistoric ethnicity (e.g., Bosselin & Djindjian 1999).

At issue fundamentally is the question of the explanation of interassemblage variability: is **any and all** variability the result and reflection of ethnicity or are only certain, specific aspects of variation among archeological remains potentially informative about style at the bounded social group level? If one accepts the existence of complex, multiple causation, then the task of teasing out what is stylistic in character (and hence - at a level beyond individual variation - potentially "ethnic" in its signaling) in the archeological record is difficult and often frustrating - but not hopeless. Such optimism tempered by realism is a hallmark of both processual and some post-processual archeology. But, in fairness to the European "side", great sophistication in terms of functional and ethnological reconstruction was independently developed by the late André Leroi-Gourhan and his "Paris" school - precisely, I think, because he came to prehistoric archeology from the social sciences, not from traditional history or geology. Other independent convergences with the multi-layered (but heavily culture-ecological) American perspective can be seen in the development of the Cambridge (or British) school of economic prehistory during the post-World War II period, especially under the leadership of the late Grahame Clark and Eric Higgs - although many of the practitioners of this school tended to concentrate on the Mesolithic and origins of the Neolithic in their actual fieldwork, perhaps because these periods are rather better represented archeologically in the British Isles than is the Upper Paleolithic, for obvious Ice Age environmental reasons. On the contrary, it is also true that at least one major American practitioner (i.e., Sackett 1999) remains wedded to the primordial importance (and reality) of not only assigning artifact assemblages to the traditional "cultural" entities (e.g., Early Magdalenian a.k.a. Badegoulian, Perigordian), but also of defining new ones (i.e., Beauronnian), despite a very sophisticated understanding of the difficulty of determining "style" among lithic artifacts. The appeal of cultural "diagnosis" - as if prehistoric "litho-cultures" were as real as diseases - can still weigh in strong on both sides of the North Atlantic! It is for these reasons (and echoing Sally Binford's cautionary footnote 1 [1972:199]) that I hesitate to speak of national schools, although by and large it is still true that many French prehistorians tend to think of the de Mortilletian/Breuilian Upper Paleolithic entities as "real" "cultures" or groups of cultures, whereas I do think that most Americans who study these things regard them as merely useful, shorthand, descriptive **constructs**, while arguing that actual ethnic units (regional/linguistic bands, etc.) might be dimly perceived at deeper levels of analysis and had existences at more realistically restricted scales of time and space than the classic "cultures".

I and others (e.g., Binford & Sabloff 1982; A.Montet-White, personal communication) believe that it is the operative definition of "culture" that is fundamentally at the heart of the paradigmatic differences between many continental Western Europeans and Americans who study the Upper (and Middle Paleolithic)(e.g., Straus 1987,1991; Clark 1991; **pace** Sackett 1991; Harrold 1991). But this does not rule out considerable methodological convergence (see Dibble & Debénath 1991) and - for example - growing agreement between certain European and American researchers on the importance of trying - with good chronometric control and analytical rigor - to reconstruct networks of social contacts in the world of the Last Glacial by delineating "circles" of shared exotica, art styles and - presumably - symbols and beliefs that perhaps did correspond to the cultural realities of interacting regional/linguistic bands within actual territories on the ground.

PIONEERS

The specific roles of several of the main early American pioneers - as collectors and/or as actual excavators - in the study of the European Upper Paleolithic are currently dealt with elsewhere (e.g., by R.White 1992 and in this volume, as well as by Petraglia & Potts n.d.), and have been the subject of several previous publications (e.g., White & Breitborde 1992; Straus 1979, 1996; Bahn & Cole 1986; Petraglia et al. 1992; Petraglia & Potts 1992). Here I want to briefly summarize some of the main activities and contributions of the first Americans (and the Canadian, Ami) to be seriously interested in this subject. The Smithsonian Institution had been acquiring European Paleolithic artifacts since the days of Edouard Lartet (1860s-1870s) and, later (early 1900s), of Denis Peyrony, as detailed by Petraglia and Potts (n.d.). This was usually done via correspondence and Americans were not active "in the field".

It was in 1912 - two years before the start of World War I - that George Grant MacCurdy and Henry Fairfield Osborn toured the Paleolithic sites of Southwest France (Périgord and Pyrenees) and Cantabrian Spain. Collections were acquired for the American Museum of Natural History, of which Osborn was Director (Bahn & Cole 1986:137). The principal site they visited in Spain was El Castillo, during its second year of actual excavation by the Institut de Paléontologie under the direction of Hugo Obermaier (Breuil & Obermaier 1913:3). No doubt as a consequence of this visit, the 1913 field crew at El Castillo included Nels Nelson, then a young curator at the American Museum who would soon thereafter apply the stratigraphic method he observed in the great Spanish cave site in his seminal excavations in the Galisteo Basin of New Mexico. Among his fellow participants on the 1913 team at El Castillo were the young scholars Miles Burkitt and Pierre Teilhard de Chardin (Breuil & Obermaier 1914). After this initial contact, the catastrophe of the Great War caused an hiatus of more than a decade in American participation in the study of the Upper Paleolithic. It was Osborn, a paleontologist and author of the popular *Men of the Old Stone Age,* who would later arrange for the 1924 publication of an English translation of Obermaier's *El Hombre Fósil* by Yale for the Hispanic Society of America, of which he was Vice President.

MacCurdy 's American School in France (later the ASPR, affiliated with the Archaeological Institute of America, which has traditionally been involved in classical archeology) began its work in 1921 digging for several weeks at the classic site of La Quina (Charente), with the support of Dr. Henri-Martin. They also visited many Upper Paleolithic cave art and residential sites in northern Aquitaine and in the Pyrenees and - in a practice they were to continue in following years - at several sites they dug for a half day to "several afternoons"(!) (MacCurdy 1922). MacCurdy's most important excavation, however, was at l'Abri des Merveilles (Castel-Merle, Dordogne), beginning in 1924: Mousterian and Aurignacian **sensu lato** (MacCurdy 1931). The School also travelled outside France and dug briefly at sites such as Dolni Vestonice and Pekarna in Czechoslovakia (MacCurdy 1927). Such "guest excavations" were generally arranged by the local specialists, with whom MacCurdy (or the Czech-American, Ales Hrdlicka, who ran the School in 1923 [Carroll 1925]) had made acquaintance (in the Moravian case, this was Karel Absolon). An example was one of the few inter-war American forays into Spanish prehistory: the visit of the ASPR in 1930 to Cantabria, where they dug for three days in a Magdalenian layer of the cave of El Pendo under the direction of the site's excavator, Father Jesús Carballo (Carballo 1931). During their brief "dig", the students (who included Sol Tax, then a student at the University of Wisconsin) uncovered one of the many famous portable art objects from El Pendo: a perforated flat bone ("churinga") with engraved images of a stag and a fish (see Corchón 1986:424 & fig.166.3). MacCurdy and his group visited other sites and museums in Spain in the inter-war period, guided by Obermaier, the Conde de la Vega del Sella and the Marqués de Cerralbo (Straus 1979). In 1924 he published *Human Origins: A Manuel of Prehistory*. Small numbers of Spanish artifacts (from such classic sites as Altamira, Castillo, Morín) made there way through purchase or donation into the Smithsonian, Field and Harvard Peabody museums; Carballo was sometimes the source thereof (Straus 1996). The Old Stone Age of the Old World was now on the curriculum in the New! But doing prehistory 1920s-style could today be seen as an exotic, somewhat muscular form of genteel art collection by an elite few Americans, with a notable emphasis on spectacular or unusual finds.

The French-Canadian, Henri-Marc Ami, who had already acquired vast collections of French materials, excavated at the famous site of Combe-Capelle Bas (Dordogne) between 1926-1931 with the strong support of Denis Peyrony (Dibble & Lenoir 1995:21; R. White 1988 and personal communication). This is a Mousterian site, but it is adjacent to the (infamous) site of Roc de Combe-Capelle, itself with a nearly full Upper Paleolithic sequence. In 1927, Pond and Collie, who also acquired large French collections for the Logan Museum, excavated at Abri Cellier (Le Ruth, Dordogne), an Aurignacian site (White & Breitborde 1992). In the same year and in 1928-29, Henry Field (grand-nephew of the founder of the Field Museum of Natural History, Marshall Field, and himself at the time the Museum's Assistant Curator of Physical Anthropology, went on buying trips to France, assisted by the Abbé Breuil. He acquired more than 120,000 artifacts according to Bahn and Cole (1986:96). The romantic adventure aspects of doing prehistoric archeology in Europe during this period is best captured by the book, *Primitive Hearths in the Pyrenees: The Story of a Summer's Exploration in the Haunts of Prehistoric Man*, by Ruth Sawtell and Ida Treat (1927). Although they also reported on their excavation at the Azilian site of the Trou Violet (Ariège) in the more scientific outlet of *L'Anthropologie* (Vaillant-Couturier Treat & Vaillant-Couturier 1928), the flavor and spirit of what an "expedition" was like is deliciously recounted in this part-travelogue, part-dig journal, part-prehistory text book. And, as luck would have it, they uncovered one

of the few known human burials from the Azilian period! As the authors make clear, they were far from alone; many others (French and foreigners) were busy digging away at the fertile cave deposits of southern France. All knew one another and visited from site to site to exchange impressions...and finds.

The Ariège-Haute Garonne sector of the Pyrenees was also the venue for one of the last American expeditions before the Second World War, that of J.Townsend Russell in association with Comte Henri Bégouën. The so-called Franco-American Union for Prehistoric Research - formed through an agreement between the Smithsonian and the Université de Toulouse and supported by the Old World Archaeology Fund of which Russell, an honorary "Collaborator in Old World Archaeology" at the U.S. National Museum, was a major donor - conducted two months of excavations in 1931 at the nearby, classic sites of Marsoulas, Tarté and Roquecourbère (open-air quarry/workshop) (Russell 1932; Bégouën & Russell 1933). The collections were divided by contract between Toulouse and Washington; they have respectively been the objects of recent studies by Foucher and San Juan (2000 and in preparation) and by Petraglia, Potts, Straus and Vandiver (n.d.). Note that large collections of Jean Cazedessus from Roquecourbère Cave had earlier been sold to Field, although Bégouën had managed to save a spectacular series of Solutrean points for the Toulouse Natural History Museum (Bahn & Cole 1986:100; Foucher & San Juan 2000:199). Russell, who was independently wealthy, was part of the small coterie of Americans involved in prehistoric studies in Europe and had been associated with MacCurdy's American School. The elite nature of such activities as visiting sites in France and even more exotic parts of Europe and the Near East, buying collections from European prehistorians of often modest means (including teachers like Cazedessus), trying one's hand at actually digging for more-or-less short periods of time, donating one's time, knowledge and money to prestigious American museums, and associating with influential foreign and U.S. scholars (e.g., Breuil, Bégouën, Absolon, Garrod, MacCurdy, Osborn, Hrdlicka) is clear; it was a socially very acceptable pursuit for intellectually inclined persons of means. The term **dilettante** in its full sense would not seem to be an unfair characterization of this kind of early American prehistorian. (A major exception, of course, was the American expatriate, Harper Kelley, a World War I veteran who had returned to France with MacCurdy's ASPR, studied with (and later became a very close friend and associate of) Breuil and became the Curator of Paleolithic collections at the Musée de l'Homme in Paris. A specialist in Lower Paleolithic stone tools, Kelley would end his career in the years after World War II as a Research Director in the CNRS [Ripoll 1994:153].)

Otherwise the activity of Americans visiting Europe to "do" prehistory ground and finally crashed to a halt with the onset of the Great Depression and then the successive outbreaks of the Spanish Civil War and World War II. The stage, however, was set for a more scientific, rigorous prehistoric archeology after the new debacle.

MOVIUS

In the period immediately succeeding the Second World War, American archeologists and human paleontologists - now often with major financial support from the U.S. Government's National Science Foundation - became much more numerous and active throughout the Old World - particularly in Europe. New contacts were made, sites visited and collections studied and interpreted from new perspectives. Prominent among these was F.Clark Howell, whose Lower Paleolithic excavations at Torralba and Ambrona would be responsible for activating major American interest in the full range of the Stone Age in Spain, centered on the University of Chicago. However, In terms of the study of the Upper Paleolithic, undoubtedly the central American figure in the decades immediately after World War II was MacCurdy's student Hallam L. Movius of Harvard, who was earlier well- known for his research on the Lower Paleolithic of East Asia and the late Mesolithic of Ireland. After a "trial" excavation at La Colombière in eastern France (and whose chronology would controversial: Perigordian or early Magdalenian) (Movius & Judson 1956; cf. Desbrosse 1976), Movius focused the rest of his career on the methodologically sophisticated excavation, analysis and publication of l'Abri Pataud in the center of Les Eyzies.

After testing in 1953, the site was actually purchased by Harvard (Peabody Museum) and then donated to the French Government (Musée de l'Homme) in exchange for a 20-year exclusive excavation permit. The Pataud excavations (1958-64) became a Mecca for American (and other) students of prehistory, many of whom (in addition to Bricker, Brooks, Clay, David and Sackett) would go on to become major figures in that or other areas of archeology or anthropology (e.g., Keith Basso, Alan Bilsborough, C.L.Brace,

K.C.Chang, Sonia Cole, Joakim Hahn, Karl Heider, Cynthia Irwin, G.Ll.Isaac, W. von Koenigswald, R. Paepe, Ralph Rowlett, Sally Schanfield (Binford), James Stoltman, Mariella Taschini, John Terrell, Robert Whallon, et al.) (Movius 1975). Although Movius' overriding goals were chronostratigraphic and classificatory in nature (i.e., to understand and resolve the definitional problems of the Aurignaco-Perigordian systematics as proposed in the 1930s by Denis Peyrony as a revision of Breuil's classic scheme of 1912), the Pataud excavation would be a seminal project in terms of 1.) new, rigorous excavation and recording techniques; 2.) a fresh approach to rockshelter/cave mouth sedimentological interpretation (William Farrand), 3.) the systematic application of radiocarbon, a dating method for the Upper Paleolithic independent of the artifacts themselves; 4.) paleoecological modeling (Joan Wilson); 5.) flint sourcing (Bricker); 6.) objectified, metric (but pre-PC) attribute analysis for the classification of artifacts (Movius and his principal students - Bricker, Brooks, Clay, David - each of whom would write a dissertation on a particular techo-complex or industrial phase); 7.) site structure analyses focusing on the role of hearths (Movius); 8.) paleontological **and**, later, archeozoological analyses of the faunal assemblages, including determination of seasonality and hunting practices (Bouchud; Spiess [1979]); and 9.) a monumental, profusely illustrated, multi-volume series of multi-disciplinary monographs of the highest quality, both in English (*Excavation of the Abri Pataud*, H.L. Movius, General Editor) and, after Movius' death, in French (*Le Paléolithique Supérieur de l'Abri Pataud: Les Fouilles de H.L.Movius*, H.M.Bricker, Editor), as well as a very interesting, synthetic, retrospective article by Movius (1974). Heavily descriptive as the monographs (published as Bulletins 30, 31, 34, 37 of the ASPR) and many attribute analysis articles produced by Movius and his students were, they set a new standard for the full publication of Paleolithic sites that is still rarely equalled. Certainly, compared to the frequent amateurism and lack of substantive (or any) publication of many excavations in the pre-WWII period, the Pataud publications (full references in Bricker 1995) represented a turning point in the professionalization of prehistoric archeology, as were Movius's standards for excavation and analysis - supported as they were by substantial, long-term, institutional funding.

Now, of course, none of this was occurring in a void. Taking the lead as usual, the French in the post-WWII decades were creating CNRS laboratories dedicated to prehistoric archeological and Quaternary research, most importantly at the Université de Bordeaux (under the direction of François Bordes in collaboration with Denise de Sonneville-Bordes) and at the Sorbonne (under the direction of André Leroi-Gourhan in collaboration with Arlette Leroi-Gourhan). They would train most of the next generation of French prehistorians, as well as many foreigner specialists. These two centers, located in regions with rather different main types of Paleolithic sites (rockshelters versus open-air loci), took somewhat different tacks in the study of the Stone Age prehistory: geological and typological at Bordeaux versus paleoethnological and technological at Paris. Thus there was considerable convergence of problem-orientation and methods between the Movius and Bordes groups and approaches, but important, though at first rather latent points of common interest in terms of reconstructing past environments and human behaviors between the Americans and the Leroi-Gourhan "school". Other parallelisms to the "anthropological" view of what could be gleaned from archeology were also developing in Britain, with Grahame Clark's creation of a school of "economic prehistory: at Cambridge in the early post-WWII period (notably with the excavation of the early Mesolithic site of Star Carr). Ironically, it would be Bordes, the non-anthropological geologist by training - sporting a love/hate relationship with America and Americans - who most engaged the U.S. archeological community and popularized (his version of) the European Paleolithic in America, through his lecture tours, English-language books *The Old Stone Age* (1968) and *A Tale of Two Caves* (1972), and especially because of his long, spirited debate with Lewis and Sally Binford over the significance of Mousterian inter-assemblage ("facies") variability.

Just prior to the outbreak of the great theoretical debate was published one of the most substantive works on an aspect of the European Upper Paleolithic ever to be produced by a single North American: *Le Solutréen en France* by the Philip E.L. Smith (1966). This Canadian student of Movius had gone to France to study the composition, nature and origins of the Solutrean phenomenon and quickly got the trust of Bordes, who charged him with supervisng his stratigraphic re-excavation of the type-site of Laugerie-Haute (Les Eyzies) in 1957. Despite the traditionally "phylogenetic" nature of Smith's **magnum opus**, he brought to the subject the latest in 1950s-early 1960s American anthropological theory (e.g., Krieger, Kroeber, Kluckhohn, Taylor, White, Willey and Phillips) and produced a work that

empirically remains **the** reference work on the Solutrean in France. Bricker (who has spent his professional career at Tulane University in New Orleans) later excavated the Chatelperronian site of Les Tambourets in collaboration with Henri Laville in the upper Garonne valley near the edge of the Pyrenees; his student, Gail L. Peterkin went on to do a dissertation on Upper Paleolithic hunting technology in France.

THE MEANING OF UPPER PALEOLITHIC INTER-ASSEMBLAGE VARIABILITY

The Bordes-Binford debate was specifically on the Mousterian and reproduced itself among 2-3 successive generations of prehistoric archeologists, both French and Anglo-Canadian-American (the latter notably including P.Mellars, N.Rolland, L.G.Freeman, H.Dibble, M.Barton, S.Kuhn, et al.), as well as numerous archeozoologists stimulated (favorably or negatively) by Binford's ideas about Neandertal subsistence. This enormously productive, stimulating, but **per se** ultimately inconclusive debate also spun off considerable interest and activity in the study of **Upper Paleolithic** inter-assemblage variability. The crystallization of a holistic inter-disciplinary field of "paleoanthropology" by J. Desmond Clark and F.Clark Howell in their Special Issue of the *American Anthropologist* (1966) focused both on the elaboration of the empirical record of hominid evolution and on issues of function and style in artifact assemblage variation. This was followed two years later by the Binfords' epochal collection of processual case studies, *New Perspectives in Archeology* (1968). Although both volumes included papers on Upper Paleolithic endscraper variability by James Sackett derived from his Movius-directed Harvard dissertation, the "new archeology" take on the Old Stone Age tended to be dominated by young faculty and graduate students at two Midwestern universities: Michigan and Chicago. In the late 1960s-1970s the center of gravity within the small, but growing community of American prehistorians involved in the European Paleolithic from an explicitly **anthropological** perspective moved away from the old elite institutions of the East Coast, and it kept on moving west toward New Mexico, Arizona, California and Washington State in following years - in large part because of Lewis Binford. Sackett spent his professional career at the University of California at

Los Angeles and excavated the large, complex, open-air Upper Paleolithic site of Solvieux in very close collaboration with the late Jean Gaussen, becoming one of the most thoroughly "French" of the American archeologists in his perspective and approach to the subject. Collaborating with Henri Laville and Jean-Philippe Rigaud, Sackett helped produce the definitive statement of the "Bordesian" view of the Middle and Upper Paleolithic prehistory of southwest France: *Rockshelters of the Perigord* in 1980, albeit with considerable hints of dissention concerning a strict phylogenetic or "stylistic" interpretation of Perigordian and Magdalenian systematics. Sackett's student, Linda Grimm, would study a new "culture" that he defined at Solvieux, the Beauronnian.

The Michigan group included Arthur Jelinek, Anta Montet-White. The Chicago group that later formed around Howell and Binford there included (among others who would mainly work in the Lower Paleolithic) Richard Klein, Robert Whallon and Freeman, who in turn trained G.A.Clark, Frank Harrold, Margaret Conkey and me.

Montet-White, who is French and received a Doctorat d'Etat from Bordeaux, but studied at Michigan when Binford was also there and was clearly influenced by American anthropological archeology (Spaulding, Griffin), became one of the most geographically extensive and fieldwork-oriented of the "Americans" to study the European Upper Paleolithic. During her long research career she has directed excavations in France (Le Malpas rockshelter and, more recently at Solutré), at several sites in Bosnia, at Spadzista in Krakow (Poland) and at Grubgraben (Austria), always taking a broadly anthropological, culture-ecological perspective, with a particular focus on hunter-gatherer patterns of mobility, as reflected in lithic raw material procurement and hunting practices. Among her students at the University of Kansas, Dixie West has done interesting studies of the controversial issue of human exploitation of mammoths in the Upper Paleolithic of Central Europe. Jelinek, of course, concentrated his Old World research efforts on the Middle Paleolithic of Israel (Tabun Cave) and southwest France (La Quina), with an emphasis on variability and change among artifact assemblages, in part reflecting patterns of retouching, reuse and recycling that so influenced his student Dibble, who has also focused on the Middle Paleolithic of France. Klein analyzed Upper (and Middle) Paleolithic materials from Ukraine and southern Russia for his dissertation at Chicago, making this extraordinary record easily accessible to a Western readership for

the first time in two important books, before moving the focus of his research to southern Africa. Conscientiously following in Klein's Russian footsteps has been John Hoffecker. Whallon conducted several surveys and Upper Paleolithic excavations in Serbia and Montenegro. His student at Michigan, Michael Jochim, has had a long career assiduously surveying and excavating sites pertaining to the terminal Paleolithic and especially Mesolithic in southern Germany. It has been Jochim who has most explicitly and in greatest detail outlined the culture-ecological approach to doing the anthropological archeology of Stone Age hunter-gatherers, in books that have drawn heavily on the literatures of the ethnography of foragers and economic modeling. An influential theoretician of hunter-gatherer demograpy and social organization in relation to the European Upper Paleolithic has been H.M.Wobst, first at Michigan and later at Massachusetts.

Freeman, after working at Torralba with Howell and doing a Ph.D. on Mousterian inter-assemblage variability in Cantabrian Spain (initially taking the broadly functionalist perspective of Binford), proceeded in 1966-69 to carry out a seminal excavation in Cueva Morín near Santander with Father Joaquín González Echegaray, who is a typologist, but also an ethnographer and art historian. This model of modern excavation methods, interdisciplinary analysis and full publication, concerned a stratigraphic sequence that ran through a series of Mousterian levels through most of the Upper Paleolithic stages found in Cantabria. This project was in part specifically designed to test propositions concerning the nature of the Middle - Upper Paleolithic transition and the nature of variability among Mousterian assemblages. Morín also represented an important chapter in the development of Spanish Stone Age studies: several Spanish and American students who were to later do significant doctoral and post-doctoral research on various Paleolithic and Mesolithic techno-complexes (including G.A.Clark, M.Conkey and M.McCullough, who did a University of Pennsylvania dissertation on the Vasco-Cantabrian "Noaillan") worked on the excavation and Freeman's multi-causal approach to interassemblage variability, expertise in statistical and spatial analysis and his interest in fauna and human subsistence practices began to nudge Spanish prehistory away from complete loyalty to the French phylogenetic approach to culture-history and began to influence regional Quaternary paleontology in the direction of what would eventually be known as "archeozoology". The Morín project included Karl Butzer, who brought an explicitly geomorphological and culture-ecological approach to the study of the Cantabrian Paleolithic in the context of fluctuating Upper Pleistocene environments. Late taking up again the work initiated in the 1950s by Paul Janssens and González Echegaray in the Cave of El Juyo, also near Santander, Freeman and Echegaray concentrated their new (recently concluded) excavations on broad area excavation and the documentation of mid-Magdalenian structures, as well as on the application of an intensive program of flotation and "total" recovery. This work continues Freeman's interest in Paleolithic diet. Finally, the team of González Echegaray and Freeman has taken novel approaches to the interpretation of cave art, especially at Altamira. As in their archeological excavations, this duo combines González Echegaray's classic (but open-minded) approach to cave art (e.g., dating by style, comparative analysis) with Freeman's eclectic interests in ethology, psychology and religion. This collaboration, which has now lasted some 35 years, works precisely because Freeman's and González Echegaray's interests and skills are complementary, each bringing different but mutually respected perspectives to the interpretation of the remote past.

Freeman's students have gone on to do a variety of things related to the Stone Age, but always taking a multi-causal, anthropological perspective to their work. The "Chicago" impact in Spain has been significant and long-lived. Geoffrey Clark studied the Asturian Mesolithic from a rigorously chronometric, statistical, functional and subsistence point of view. More recently he has conducted large surveys and excavations (especially in Mousterian deposits) in Jordan. He and Straus conducted one of the first systematic pedestrian surveys to be done in Spain (in northern Burgos in 1972) and then excavated La Riera Cave, taking an explicitly scientific (hypothesis testing) approach to the interpretation of Upper Paleolithic assemblage variability, especially in relationship to evidence to changes and differences in human subsistence activities, with a heavy emphasis on the use of radiocarbon to control for time independently of artifacts. The result was a monograph that attempted to be synthetically interdisciplinary in character, while presenting the compete corpus of recovered data. Straus, after a 1975 dissertation that explicitly sought to define and explain variability among Solutrean artifact and faunal assemblages (and after the La Riera Paleoecological Project), has gone on to excavate numerous sites in France, Portugal, Belgium and currently again in Spain. These projects (notably l'Abri Dufaure in Les Landes, Casa da Moura in Estremadura, Vidigal in Alentejo, le Trou Magrite, Huccorgne, l'Abri du Pape and la Grotte du Bois Laiterie in Wallonia, and la Cueva del Mirón in Cantabria) approached the archeological record of the Upper Paleolithic as laboratories for understanding differences and similarities in terms of human activities among sites and regions, as well as for understanding changes through time as they developed in response to changing environmental and demographic conditions. A broadly comparative, culture-ecological approach has been taken, as opposed to a culture-historical one, although Straus has collaborated with a variety of European researchers who often take a decidedly more traditional approach to the record, while often proposing novel hypotheses of their own which Straus has attempted to test by bringing fresh data to bear. Such collaborations have included the late Robert Arambourou, Joao Zilhao, Marcel Otte, and currently (as at La Riera in the mid-late 1970s) Manuel González Morales. In addition, close, long-standing collaborations with the late Henri Laville (sedimentologist) and Jesús Altuna (paleontologist) have been extremely productive, despite disciplinary differences.

Other Freeman students included Francis Harrold, who did widely cited synthetic studies of the Chatelperronian and recently exavated Epigravettian levels in Konispol Cave in Albania, as well as collaborating with geologist Brooks Ellwood on a vast project of paleoclimatic reconstruction through magnetic susceptibility acrosss southern Europe; Margaret Conkey, who has concentrated the Upper Paleolithic aspects of her research on attempting to reconstruct aspects of prehistoric social and territorial organization from mobile art and on the interpretation of cave art; and, more recently, James Pokines and Heather Stettler, who used materials mainly from El Juyo to respectively study Tardiglacial habitats through raptor-deposited microfaunal remains and changes in iconography among decorated bone/antler artifacts.

In a category all by himself, science writer Alexander Marshack single-handedly revolutionized the study of (especially portable) Upper Paleolithic art, with his ground-breaking use of microscopic analysis and special lighting. His book, *The Roots of Civilization* (1972, second edition: 1991), and a myriad of articles both empirical and more speculative, opened new avenues for interpretation of this phenomenon, not only in Europe but also in the Near East and Africa, and have been followed up on by several European specialists (e.g., F.d'Errico, C.Fritz). Marshack's concern for and arguments about the origins of human notation and expression have been revolutionary, if controversial. "Outsiders" can stimulate!

The economic and social aspects of the Upper Paleolithic have been spectacularly stressed by Olga Soffer in her analyses of sites and materials (artifactual and faunal) from Russia and Central Europe. In her work she has collaborated extensively with a large number of Russian and Czech, as well as American specialists (notably James Adavasio for the study of Pavlovian nets and textiles and Pamela Vandiver for the study of Pavlovian ceramic technology, among others). Soffer's student Brian Adams has done dissertation research on the earliest Upper Paleolithic in Hungary. Other instances of fruitful, long-term American-European collaborations include the cases of Jan Simek and Jean-Philippe Rigaud (in the excavation and study of Grottes Vaufrey and XVI in Dordogne) and James Enloe with Françoise Audouze and Francine David (in the excavation and faunal analysis of Verberie in northern France). Simek (a student of Conkey) and Todd Koetje have continued working on the complex problems of spatial analysis, pioneered by Whallon and Freeman. A Canadian who has been based at New York University for many years, Randall White has concentrated his research on the earliest evidence of artistic and ornamental expression in the Périgord, a region which he knows intimately both in terms of its topography and its extraordinarily rich Upper Paleolithic record. White has recently excavated at the classic site of Castanet and he has also analyzed early works of portable art from Russia and (with Canadian Michael Bisson) the recently re-discovered "Canadian" collection of Epigravettian figurines from Grimaldi (Italian Liguria). His students (both American and Canadian), Anne Pike Tay, Heidi Knecht and Ariane Burke, have made major contributions to archeozoology and bone technology studies in the Upper (and Middle) Paleolithic of France, Spain and Ukraine. The longstanding American commitments to the Aurignacian of southwest France has recently been continued by Brook Blades, in a study focusing on lithic raw material economy. Students of Conkey - Marcia-Ann Dobres and Heather Price - did major analyses of Magdalenian worked bone/antler artifacts from the Pyrenees, the former becoming a leader in the growing study of the role of "human agency" in prehistory. Recent University of New Mexico graduates, besides Enloe, who have worked (and in some cases still do work) in the archeology of the

Upper Paleolithic include Michael Petraglia, Kaoru Akoshima, Mary Stiner, Steven Kuhn, Anna Backer and Rebecca Miller. Randall Donahue, who did a Michigan State University dissertation on Epigravettian materials in Italy, has continued to work in Italy and England from an academic position in Britain. Roy Larick studied Solutrean lithic raw material use in southwest France. C.M. Barton has developed long-term, ongoing collaborations on projects spanning the late Quaternary in southeast Spain. Several American lithic micro-wear specialists have substantively analyzed European Paleolithic and Mesolithic materials (e.g., Lawrence Keeley, Emily Moss, John Dumont, B.Hardy, S.Tomaskova, Patricia Anderson - the latter of whom is based in France). An eclectic archeologist with heavy reasearch investment in archeozoology in both the Great Basin and France and author of a superb book on *The Establishment of Human Antiquity* in 19th century Europe, Donald Grayson of the University Washington, has a fruitful, longstanding collaboration with Françoise Delpech of the Université de Bordeaux in the analysis of faunas from a number of Middle and Upper Paleolithic sites excavated by Rigaud. This list of Americans recently or currently involved in research in Europe could go on, but the point has been made: there has been an explosion of active interest since the late 1960s. The meeting of the two archeological worlds became substantive and continuous.

BY WAY OF CONCLUSION

Of course many of these North American archeologists do not work exclusively in the European Upper Paleolithic; some did dissertations but did not continue in this field; others have conducted one or a few projects in Europe; but only a few have made the European Upper Paleolithic their full-time, active research specialization and conducted multiple and/ or long-term excavations. Some very provocative ideas on the Upper Paleolithic of Europe have been published by Americans who are not Upper Paleolithic specialists (e.g., A.Gilman, E.Zubrow). The point is that fairly large numbers of researchers based in the U.S. or Canada have been stimulated to contribute to understanding human lifeways during the mid-late Last Glacial in Europe. I would argue that many or most of them - despite a wide variety of theoretical backgrounds and training experiences - have been motivated to do their research by the debates over how to explain the differences and similarities among assemblages and sites: ethnicity/ style, site role/function (including subsistence, mobility, seasonality), sampling accidents. Once the monolithic culture-historic or phylogenetic "explanation" was challenged (in large part by Americans led by the Binfords, together with Freeman and others), new perspectives were opened up, ranging from culture-ecology to social organization and territorial marking to individual human agency to gender issues to ideology and symbolism. Asking questions of this complexity generated much interest and activity in new ways in which to analyze fauna (stimulated by Binford's ethnoarcheological work especially among the Nunamiut) including butchering patterns, economic values, evidence of seasonality, etc. It also led to the development of specializations such as statistical, spatial and lithic microwear analyses, at least initially dominated by Americans. The distance of America from the subject matter may tend to allow American archeologists to try to "see the forest despite the trees", which may sometimes be hard for Europeans who may be continuously too close to the data, too concerned with description to focus on broad patterns or to seek explanations. The strengths and weaknesses of each "group" may compensate for those of the other.

It is clear that there has been substantial methodological convergence in recent decades between American and European specialists in the Upper Paleolithic. And I would argue that there is decreasing theoretical polarization as classic culture-historians become less numerous in Europe and strict functionalists dwindle in America. Europeans have gotten more and more into research that is fundamentally culture-ecological in nature (e.g., impressive archeozoological work), while Americans are exploring ways to use European data (some "hard" such as non-local lithic, shell and fossil distributions; some "soft" such as design elements and "styles" in portable or rupestral art) to get at real social units in the Upper Paleolithic. Some Americans have come to acknowledge beyond lip-service that there was more to Upper Paleolithic life that is accessible through archeology than flint-knapping and deer hunting; some Europeans have come to realize that all variation is not "ethnic" in nature. The vastly increased amount of trans-Atlantic contact and long-term interaction and collaboration over the last 35-40 years has paid off to the extent that there may soon be no strong basis for distinguishing an "American" versus a "European" perspective on the Upper Paleolithic. Plurality of views that cross-cut the ocean barrier, within a commonality of accepted "best

practices" in excavation, interdisciplinary analysis and publication, will be the order of the day - and indeed may be already. Nonetheless, the combination of European expertise and intimate familiarity with their archeological record and the ability of Americans - with their "distance" - to take the broad, fresh view, to try new ideas (often naive and wrong, but sometimes stimulating) will hopefully continue to be one of dynamic research synergy.

ACKNOWLEDGEMENTS

I wish to thank all the Spanish, French, Portuguese and Belgian colleagues who have educated and put up with me over the last 30 years. I thank my mentors, L.G.Freeman and J.González Echegary, for launching me on an international career that was predestined by my great-grandfather and grandfather (Louis and Guy Magnant), amateur prehistorians of the Charente. I apologize to all my American and Canadian colleagues whom I may have misrepresented, or, due to lack of space, to whom I may have given short shrift or left out altogether. Randy White & Anta Montet-White supplied me with information. I give references only for the earlier work, since there is no room to even begin to cite the avalanche of Americanist publications since the mid-1960s. This essay is obviously just a beginning. The long, productive interaction between North American archeologists and European prehistorians and the shifting nature of their relationship over a century should be the subjects of much further research and discussion in the future. Finally, I thank my friends Marcel Otte and Janusz Kozlowski for allowing the Commission on the Upper Paleolithic of Europe to sponsor the symposium at the XIV UISPP Congress on which this volume is based. My participation at Liège was supported by the University of New Mexico College of Arts and Sciences and *Journal of Anthropological Research*.

Department of Anthropology
University of New Mexico
Albuquerque, NM 87131 USA
lstraus@unm.edu

BIBLIOGRAPHY

BAHN, P. & COLE, G., 1986, La préhistoire pyrénéenne aux Etats-Unis. *Bulletin de la Société Préhistorique Ariège-Pyrénées* 41, p. 95-149.

BEGOUEN, H. & RUSSELL, J.T., 1932, La campagne de fouilles de 1931 à Marsoulas, Tarté et Roquecourbère. Toulouse: Edouard Privat.

BINFORD, L. & SABLOFF, J., 1982, Paradigms, systematics and archaelogy. *Journal of Anthropological Research* 38, p. 137-153.

BINFORD, S. & BINFORD, L., (Eds.), 1968, *New Perspectives in Archeology*. Chicago: Aldine.

BINFORD, S., 1972, The significance of variability: a minority report. In *The Origin of Homo sapiens*, edited by F. Bordes. Paris: UNESCO, p.199-210.

BORDES, F., 1968, *The Old Stone Age*. New York: McGraw-Hill.

_____, 1972, *A Tale of Two Caves*. New York: Harper & Row.

BOSSELIN, B. & DJINDIAN, F., 1999, Une révision de la séquence de la Riera (Asturies) et la question du Badegoulien cantabrique. *Bulletin de la Société Préhistorique Française* 96, p.153-173.

BREUIL, H. & OBERMAIER, H., 1913, Institut de Paléonologie Humaine: Travaux exécutés en 1912. *L'Anthropologie* 24, p. 1-16.

_____ & _____, 1914, Institut de Paléontologie Humaine: Travaux en Espagne. *L'Anthropologie* 25, p. 233-253.

BRICKER, H. (Ed.), 1995, *Le Paléolithique Supérieur de l'Abri Pataud: Les Fouilles de H.L.Movius, Jr.* Paris: Documents d'Archéologie Française 50.

CARROLL, M., 1925, Les Eyzies, capital of the prehistoric world. *Art and Archaeology* 19, p.115-120.

CARBALLO, J., 1931, The American School of Prehistoric Research visits the cavern of El Pendo. *Bulletin of the American School of Prehistoric Research* 7, p. 24-27.

CLARK, G.A., 1991, A paradigm is like an onion: reflections on my biases. In *Perspectives on the Past,* edited by G.A. Clark. Philadelphia: University of Pennsylvania Press, p. 79-108.

CLARK, J.D. & F.C. HOWELL (Eds.), 1966, *Recent Studies in Paleoanthropology*. American Anthropologist 68, no.2, pt.2.

CORCHON, M.S., 1986, *El Arte Mueble del Paleolítico Cantábrico*. Madrid: Centro de Investigación y Museo de Altamira Monografías 16.

DESBROSSE, R., 1976, Les civilisations du Paléolithique supérieur dans le Jura et en Franche-Comté. In *La Préhistoire Française*, edited by H.de Lumley. Paris: CNRS, p. 1348-1357.

DIBBLE, H. & DEBENATH, A., 1991, Paradigmatic differences in a collaborative research project. In *Perspectives on the Past,* edited by G.A.Clark. Philadelphia: University of Pennsylvania Press, p. 217-226.

_____ & LENOIR, M., 1995, *The Middle Paleolithic Site of Combe-Capelle Bas*. Philadelphia: University of Pennsylvania Museum.

FOUCHER, P. & SAN JUAN, C. 2000, La Grotte de Roquecourbère: ses industries lithiques solutréennes et la révision critique de son art pariétal. *Bulletin de la Société Préhistorique Française* 97, p. 199-210.

HARROLD, F., 1991, The elephant and the blind men: paradigms, data gaps and the Middle-Upper Paleolithic transition in southwestern France. In *Perspectives on the Past*, edited by G.A.Clark. Philadelphia: University of Pennsylvania Press, p. 164-182.

MACCURDY, G.G., 1922, The first season's work of the American School in France for Prehistoric Studies. *American Anthropologist* 24, p. 61-71.

_____, 1927, Report of the Director on the work of the sixty season. *Bulletin of the American School of Prehistoric Research* 3, p. 1-22.

_____, 1931, The Abri des Merveilles at Castel-Merle, near Sergeac. *Bulletin of the American School of Prehistoric Research* 7, p.12-23.

MARSHACK, A., 1972. *The Roots of Civilization*. London: Weidengeld & Nicholson.

MOVIUS, H.L., 1953, Old World prehistory. In *Anthropology Today,* edited by A.L.Kroeber. Chicago: University of Chicago Press, p. 163-192.

_____, 1974, The Abri Pataud Program of the French Upper Paleolithic in retrospect. In *Archaeological Researches in Retrospect*, edited by G.Willey. Cambridge: Winthrop, p. 87-116.

_____, (Ed.), 1975, *Excavation of the Abri Pataud, Les Eyzies*. Cambridge: Peabody Museum, Harvard. Bulletin of the American School of Prehistoric Researc 30.

_____ & JUDSON, S., 1956, The rockshelter of La Colombière. *Bulletin of the American School of the American School of Prehistoric Research* 19.

PETRAGLIA, M., POTTS, R., & VANDIVER, P., 1992, Une "palette d'artiste" du Paléolithique supérieur provenant de la Grotte de Tarté, Haute-Garonne, France. *Bulletin de la Société Préhistorique Ariège-Pyrénées* 47, p. 161-175.

_____ & _____, n.d., *The Old World Paleolithic Collections of the National Museum of Natural*

History, Smithsonian Institution. Washington: Smithsonian Contributins in Anthropology (in press).

_____, _____, STRAUS, L. & VANDIVER, P. n.d. Upper Paleolithic collections from the Salat Valley of Pyrenean France. Unpublished manuscript in possession of the authors.

RIPOLL, E., 1994, *El Abate Henri Breuil.* Madrid:Universidad Nacional de Educación a Distancia.

RUSSELL, J.T., 1932, Report on archaeological research in the foothills of the Pyrenees. *Smithsonian Miscellaneous Collections*, vol.87, no.11.

SACKETT, J., 1991, Straight archaeology French style: the phylogenetic paradigm in historic perspective. In *Perspectives on the Past*, edited by G.A.Clark. Philadelphia: University of Pennsylvania Press, p. 109-140.

_____, 1999, *The Archaeology of Solvieux.* Los Angeles:UCLA Institute of Archaeology.

SAWTELL, R.O. & TREAT, I., 1927, *Primitive Hearths in the Pyreneees.* New York: D.Appleton.

SMITH, P.E.L., 1966, *Le Solutréen en France.* Bordeaux: Delmas.

SPIESS, A., 1979, *Reindeer and Caribou Hunters. An Archaeological Study.* New York: Academic.

STRAUS, L.G., 1979, Norteamericanos en la prehistoria. In *Santander y el Nuevo Mundo.* Santander: Institución Cultural de Cantabria, p. 567-571.

_____, 1987, Paradigm lost: a personal view of the current state of Upper Paleolithic research. *Helinium* 27, p. 157-171.

_____, 1991, Paradigm found? A research agenda for study of the Upper Paleolitic and post-Paleolithic in SW Europe. In *Perspectives on the Past*, edited by G.A.Clark. Philadelphia: University of Pennsylvania Press, p. 56-78.

_____, 1996, Hugo Obermaier and the Cantabrian Solutrean. In *El Hombre Fósil 80 Años Despues*, edited by A. Moure. Santander: Universidad de Cantabria.

VAILLANT-COUTURIER TREAT, I. & VAILLANT-COUTURIER, P., 1928, La grotte azilienne du "Trou Violet" à Montardit. *L'Anthropologie* 38, p. 217-243.

WHITE, L., 1959, *The Evolution of Culture.* New York: McGraw-Hill.

WHITE, R., 1988, Objets magdaléniens provenant de l'Abri du Soucy: la collection de H.-M.Ami au Royal Ontario Museum, Toronto, Canada. *L'Anthropologie* 92, p.29-40.

_____, 1992, The history and research significance of the Logan Museum French Paleolithic collections. In *French Paleolithic Collections in the Logan Museum of Anthropology*, edited by R.White & L.Breitborde. Bulletin of the Logan Museum of Anthropology, New Series, vol.1, no.2, p.1-37.

_____ & BREITBORDE, L. (Eds.), 1992, *French Paleolithic Collections in the Logan Museum of Anthropology, Beloit College.* Bulletin of the Logan Museum of Anthropology, New Series, vol.1, no.2.

STIRRED; NOT SHAKEN.
AMERICAN INFLUENCE ON GERMAN PALAEOLITHIC RESEARCH

Martin STREET and Miriam Noël HAIDLE

Résumé: Cette communication examine le rôle des américains dans la recherche sur le Paléolithique allemand. Bien que relativement peu nombreux comparé avec ceux qui travaillent dans dáutres puys de l'Europe occidentale, on ne peut pas sous-estimer leur influence. Ceci est surtout le cas à un moment où bien des depcheurs allemands se sont devenus introspectifs dans un essai de nedéfinir l'identité de leur sujet d'étude et juste aussi au moment aì plusieurs importants postes de recherche changaient au niveau personnel.

Abstract: The paper examines the role of Americans presently conducting research into the German Paleolithic. Although perhaps relatively few individuals are active in Germany compared with the American involvement in other European countries, their potential influence on developments in German Paleolithic is not to be underestimated. This is particularly the case at a time when many German Palaeolithic researchers are themselves «looking inwards» in an attempt to redefine the identity of their subject, and when several pivotal research posts are due for changes at a personal level.

INTRODUCTION

In the informal spirit of the September 2001 U.I.S.P.P. session at Liège University chaired by Lawrence Straus, this paper will not attempt to identify or indeed quantify the influence of American archaeological theory on the German Palaeolithic research community (which has, at a personal level, ranged from obsessive adoption to passionate rejection…), but will instead attempt to present an overview of the role and nature of American involvement in the German Palaeolithic as exemplified by archaeologists of that continent actively researching in Europe.

With a few exceptions, there has been little direct American involvement in the German Palaeolithic until quite recently and there exists only a small basis upon which to evaluate the role of Americans in German Palaeolithic research. The number of American researchers in German hunter-gatherer archaeology is small but, since they come from a different research tradition, their impact in the field could nevertheless be an important one. This paper will examine whether this possible meeting of different approaches is succeeding in providing new insights into the field of German Palaeolithic and Mesolithic research.

The small number of Americans conducting research in Germany allows them to be enumerated in detail, without wishing to suggest that the following list is necessarily exhaustive. In order to fully respect the thematic potential and expand the database, the Mesolithic period was also taken under consideration and not only US citizens, but also researchers from other parts of North America were included. This expansion allows a clearer recognition of the tendencies which define the "American" influence on German Palaeolithic and Mesolithic research.

Nicholas J. Conard wrote his Ph.D. dissertation on the subject of the Middle Palaeolithic site of Tönchesberg, which he himself had excavated (Conard 1992). He continued his investigations into the Rhineland Middle Palaeolithic as Humboldt Scholar at the Neuwied based Forschungsbereich Altsteinzeit of the Römisch-Germanisches Zentralmuseums Mainz (Conard & Kandel 1997). In 1995 Conard was appointed Professor at the Tübingen University Institut für Ur- und Frühgeschichte und Archäologie des Mittelalters, where he has since further widened his studies into the Middle Palaeolithic and continued the Tübingen excavations at the Upper Palaeolithic Hohle Fels (Conard & Floss 1999, 2000) and Geissenklösterle sites. He also conducts research projects in southern Africa and Syria.

Lynn Fisher studied for several semesters at the Tübingen University Institut für Urgeschichte (today the Institut für Ur- und Frühgeschichte und

Archäologie des Mittelalters) during the preparation of her dissertation. For many years she has worked together with M. Jochim on the Mesolithic Federsee site (Fisher in press; Jochim *et al.* 1998; Noone *et al.* 1997). Her dissertation was honoured with the 3rd Tübingen Research Prize for a work on Earlier Prehistory or Quaternary Ecological Research. She is now planning further projects.

Margaret Glass, Arizona State University, Tempe, studied for some time with H.-P. Uerpmann at the Tübingen Institut für Urgeschichte while working on her dissertation about animal domestication in Europe. Parallel to this she was involved in the Federsee Project led by M. Jochim (Jochim *et al.* 1998; Noone *et al.* 1997) and taught classes at the Tübingen institute.

Paul Goldberg (Boston University) is investigating cave sedimentology at the Hohle Fels site in the context of excavations carried out by the Tübingen University Institut für Ur- und Frühgeschichte und Archäologie des Mittelalters under the directorship of N. J. Conard and H.-P. Uerpmann.

Susan Harris studied one year at the Tübingen University Institut für Urgeschichte and is today conducting research for a Ph.D. at the University of California at Santa Barbara. Her dissertation about her work on Mesolithic material (Harris & Jochim 1997) is nearing completion.

Michael Jochim, University of California at Santa Barbara, has conducted research into the Mesolithic of the Federsee region over many years (Harris & Jochim 1997; Jochim 1993, 2000; Jochim *et al.* 1998; Noone *et al.*1997).

Sam Mallin (York University, Toronto), is a Canadian researcher at present investigating the *art mobilier* (*Kleinkunst*) from sites in the Swabian Alb using a philosophical body hermeneutics approach.

Peter McCartney, Arizona State University, Tempe, was involved in the Federsee Project led by M. Jochim (Jochim *et al.* 1998; Noone *et al.* 1997).

Ann Miller finished her studies at the Tübingen University Institut für Ur- und Frühgeschichte und Archäologie des Mittelalters with an M.A. analysing the fauna from the Mesolithic site Rottenburg-Siebenlinden (Kieselbach *et al.* 2000; Miller 1998).

Laura Niven's Ph.D. research at the Tübingen Institut für Ur- und Frühgeschichte und Archäologie des Mittelalters is concerned with the fauna from Aurignacian levels at the Vogelherd cave site (Niven in press).

Linda Owen studied at the Tübingen University Institut für Urgeschichte, obtaining an M.A. with research into material from the Arctic (Owen 1984). Her subsequent doctoral research compared the micro-blade assemblages from arctic and German Upper Palaeolithic contexts (Owen 1988). Her work at Tübingen has covered trace wear analysis (Owen & Unrath 1986), composition of reference dictionaries for prehistorians (e.g. Owen 1996) and studies of gender and ethnological analogy (Owen & Porr 1999). At present she is taking a second degree (Habilitation) at Tübingen (Owen in prep.) under a scholarship of the Deutsche Forschungsgemeinschaft (DFG) and teaches in Tübingen and Berlin.

Tim Prindiville finished his studies at the Tübingen University Institut für Ur- und Frühgeschichte und Archäologie des Mittelalters with an M.A. on aspects of the Middle Palaeolithic site Wallertheim (Prindiville 2000).

Jack Rink, McMaster University at Hamilton, Ontario, Canada, is involved with the dating of the Hohle Fels cave site in the context of excavations carried out by the Tübingen University Institut für Ur- und Frühgeschichte und Archäologie des Mittelalters under the directorship of N. J. Conard and H.-P. Uerpmann. He also teaches classes at the Tübingen institute.

Fred Smith, physical anthropologist at the Northern Illinois University, DeKalb, has long had contacts with the Tübingen University Osteological Collection. He analysed the Stetten human remains from the Aurignacian levels at the Vogelherd cave site (Churchill & Smith 2000a, b) and is now examining the newly (re-)discovered Neanderthal remains from the eponymous site near Dusseldorf. At present he is Humboldt Scholar at the Institut für Ur- und Frühgeschichte und Archäologie des Mittelalters and also teaches classes in palaeoanthropology at the Tübingen institute.

Jacobo Weinstock, from Mexico, obtained his Ph.D. at the Tübingen institute under H.-P. Uerpmann on the subject of reindeer populations during the Upper Palaeolithic of western and central Europe. The dissertation was honoured with the 1st Tübingen Research Prize for a work on Earlier Prehistory or Quaternary Ecological Research.

American involvement in German Palaeolithic research has so far been concentrated on a few regional and chronological aspects of the subject, such as the Rhineland Middle Palaeolithic, the Upper Palaeolithic of southwest Germany and the Mesolithic in the foothills of the Alps.

Middle Palaeolithic	Conard, Prindiville, Smith
Upper Palaeolithic	Conard, Goldberg, Mallin, Niven, Owen, Rink, Smith, Weinstock
Mesolithic	Fisher, Glass, Harris, Jochim, McCartney, Miller

Thematically, the work of American researchers in Germany has often been oriented towards material-based analyses, influenced by processual archaeology, and thus not very different from the investigations of their German colleagues.

At an institutional level it is possible to distinguish three main groups of American researchers working on German hunter-gatherer prehistory:

A: Those with connections to the earlier Institut für Urgeschichte (Institute for Prehistory) at the University of Tübingen, studying and qualifying with H. Müller-Beck, J. Hahn und H.-P. Uerpmann (Fisher, Glass, Harris, Miller, Owen, Weinstock). Certain of these researchers were involved in Tübingen research projects.

B: Those with connections to the present Institut für Ur- und Frühgeschichte und Archäologie des Mittelalters (Institute for Pre- and Protohistory and Mediaeval Archaeology) and involvement in projects led by N. J. Conard und H.-P. Uerpmann (Niven, Prindiville, Goldberg, Rink).

C: Those in the research group of M. A. Jochim (Fisher, Glass, Harris, McCartney) investigating the Mesolithic of the Alpine foothills.

Otherwise, only isolated researchers can be identified (Smith, Mallin).

Research cooperation can be seen to be closely linked to individuals, whether as persons or institutions. Only very few "established" American senior researchers choose to come to Germany to pursue their own projects or research questions (exceptions are M. Jochim, S. Mallin and, most recently, L. Fisher). Egalitarian participation in jointly conceived projects, such as that of F. Smith in the Neandertal project, is rather uncommon. More often, American participation is in the form of clearly delimited specific analyses with larger overall projects (Goldberg, Rink).

A large number of the Americans involved in German research have / had already made first contact with Germany during their early studies (Harris, Miller, Owen, Prindiville) or, somewhat later, in the course of their doctoral research, whether as independently conceived projects (Conard) or as participants in existing projects (Fisher, Glass, Harris, McCartney, Niven, Weinstock). Subsequent to these activities, many of the researchers have established themselves professionally in Germany, the United Kingdom or the USA. Nicholas Conard and Linda Owen are today German residents and influence the course of German Palaeolithic research "from the inside out", e.g. by the introduction and coverage of thematic areas not typically treated by German prehistorians, or by establishing international research projets based at German institutions. Many of the Americans conducting research in Germany have also taken on teaching commitments at German universities.

GERMAN PALAEOLITHIC RESEARCH: A SITUATION ANALYSIS

It may be useful to describe briefly some characteristics of German Palaeolithic research to serve as background to the discussion of the role of American Palaeolithic researchers in a specifically European setting and especially to the question why there are so few American senior researcher engaged in German Palaeolthic and Mesolithic.

At the beginning of the last century the Roman German Commission decided that Palaeolithic research was not a subject with which it should be concerned. To the present day, Palaeolithic and Mesolithic archaeology are not closely identified with other areas of protohistoric and historic archaeology. These latter fields, particularly the archaeology of the Bronze and Iron Age, sometimes appear to still have an "antiquarian" flavour. A negative result of this is that Palaeolithic researchers are very rarely considered as candidates for most archaeological professorial chairs. There are only four universities with a Chair in the Palaeolithic – Cologne, Erlangen, Jena and Tübingen – the latter now in fact occupied by an American. Additionally, some Palaeolithic archaeology is taught in Greifswald and Hamburg. Furthermore, the Palaeolithic is not formally represented in the upper hierarchy of German archaeological bodies such as the regional umbrella organisations (Spatz 2002). The heterogeneity of the Antiquities Protection laws (which form the basis for these different organisations) in the various Federal states is another divisive factor.

On the other hand, while Palaeolithic researchers are not seen as forming part of the humanities tradition of archaeology, neither are they often regarded as truly "scientific" researchers. This applies even though they frequently apply scientific methodology or borrow from the social and anthropological sciences. A negative effect of this classification is that German Palaeolithic researchers are not in a position to apply for major European Union funding available in the context of the "hard" biological and physical sciences. Projects therefore tend to be very modest in scope. An additional factor is the almost universal adoption of English as the *lingua franca* of our subject. German researchers generally have no problem with the English language but publications in their native language generally have no international recognition or impact. An increasing effect of this is for example a diminished presence of German Palaeolithic research on the World Wide Web (Eriksen 2002). Linguistic isolation is, of course, not only a problem for the German-speaking world. In an investigation of journal publications, Kristian Kristansen (2001) identified the increase in such "islands of knowledge" across Europe. References in other languages were rarely quoted, finds from other countries are compared in only few cases, foreign ideas or initiatives are seldom recognised.

Furthermore, there is a general lack of profile in the public eye – popular media tend to present other, high profile non-archaeological research (for example on genetic analysis). What popular archaeological exposure does exist is very often in the form of imported foreign productions (for example BBC TV films and German translations of Anglo-American popular science publications) (Haidle 2002a). Any exceptions tend to be written by professional journalists rather than by archaeologists themselves. This possibly still reflects a typical academic "ivory tower mentality", today less common elsewhere. All these factors have, during the last few years, led to what might be described as a crisis of identity among many, particularly younger, German Palaeolithic researchers. A discussion of these issues was even the subject of a special session at the Hugo Obermaier Society annual meeting of Quaternary archaeological and other researchers in April 2001 (Haidle 2002b; Haidle *et al.* 2002; Pasda 2002; Stephan 2002; Tromnau 2002; Ziegler 2002).

Among the strengths of German Palaeolithic research are certainly the conduct and exhaustive presentation of highly detailed, excavation- or material-based analyses (Eriksen 2002). A negative corollary of this might be the general lack of a theoretical superstructure; research tends to progress not as a means to an end but as an end in itself (Gaudzinski 2002; Kind 2002). There is a clear difference here to the American or perhaps generally Anglo-Saxon / anglophone approach, which may be relevant to our discussion.

American Palaeolithic researchers can find without difficulty only relatively few opportunities for a dialogue with German researchers, limited to certain universities and other research institutes. The authorities with responsibility for recording, conservation, protection and excavation (*Denkmalschutzbehörden*) are differently organised in various regions of the Federal State. Structures are often less than transparent and Palaeolithic specialists few and far between. Additionally, until the fall of the Berlin Wall, Eastern Germany was practically inaccessible to American researchers. Upon reunification many former organisations were restructured and numerous archaeologists from the west of Germany found (temporary or permanent) employment in the new Federal States, necessitating their integration into the newly emergent regional bureaucracy. Compared with this sometimes difficult situation, American researchers would probably have found far less complicated possibilities for cooperative projects in many of the earlier Warsaw Pact countries.

In the face of these various limitations and difficulties, in those cases where research facilities are more accessible, it has indeed been possible for fruitful contacts to take place and for cooperation between American and German colleagues to develop. One example is the interest and involvement of a number of German researchers in North American projects (Müller-Beck, Hahn, Uerpmann at Tübingen), which resulted in several transatlantic students and doctoral candidates being reciprocally attracted to undertake a stay in Germany. Equally, the possibility of an extended residence at a German institute (RGZM, Neuwied) able to provide active logistical support, with access to research material and scientific literature, and possibilities for a dialogue with German colleagues, was probably an element in N. Conard's choice of research project (Rhineland Middle Palaeolithic), leading eventually to the situation today, where an American has been awarded the Chair of Prehistory at Tübingen previously occupied by H. Müller-Beck. One might say that the wheel has come full circle.

CONCLUSIONS

As stated before, perhaps due to different analytical approaches and almost certainly due to Germany's relatively few academic facilities with a tradition of Palaeolithic research, there has until now been little direct American involvement in the German Palaeolithic. It may be that this will now begin to change as a result of the identity crisis referred to above, the increasing speed of information exchange via electronic media and, not least, due to a number of past and imminent personnel changes in the occupation of key German Palaeolithic posts.

Dr. Martin Street
Römisch-Germanisches Zentralmuseum Mainz
Forschungsbereich Altsteinzeit Schloss Monrepos
56567 Neuwied, GERMANY
mjs.monrepos@rz-online.de

Dr. Miriam Noël Haidle
Institut für Ur- und Frühgeschichte und Archäologie des Mittelalters
Abt. Ältere Urgeschichte und Quartärökologie
Schloss, Burgsteige 11
72070 Tübingen GERMANY
miriam.haidle@uni-tuebingen.de

This paper was based on an extra-plenary session organised by MNH at the April 2001 HOT meeting in Halle, and a paper "German Palaeolithic research in a crisis?" presented by MS in the session "The role of Americans in the study of the European Upper Paleolithic" at the September 2001 UISPP meeting in Liège.

BIBLIOGRAPHY

CHURCHILL, S. E. & SMITH, F. H., 2000a, A modern human humerus from the early Aurignacian of Vogelherdhöhle (Stetten, Germany). *American Journal of Physical Anthropology* 112/2, p. 251-273.

CHURCHILL, S. E. & SMITH, F. H., 2000b, Makers of the early Aurignacian in Europe. *American Journal of Physical Anthropology* 113/S31, p. 61-115.

CONARD, N. J. & FLOSS, H., 1999, Ein bemalter Stein vom Hohle Fels bei Schelklingen und die Frage nach paläolithischer Höhlenkunst in Mitteleuropa. *Archäologisches Korrespondenzblatt* 29(3), p. 307-316.

CONARD, N. J. & FLOSS, H., 2000, Eine Elfenbeinplastik des Hohle Fels bei Schelklingen und ihre Bedeutung für die Entwicklung des Jungpakäolithikums in Südwestdeutschland. *Archäologisches Korrespondenzblatt* 30(4), p. 473-480.

CONARD, N. J. & KANDEL, A. W. (eds.), 1997, *Reports for the second Wallertheim workshop.* Unpublished manuscripts, Institut für Ur- und Frühgeschichte, University of Tübingen.

CONARD, N. J., 1992, *Tönchesberg and its position in the Paleolithic prehistory of Northern Europe.* Römisch-Germanisches Zentralmuseum, Forschungsinstitut für Vor- und Frühgeschichte Monographien Vol.20. Bonn: Rudolf Habelt.

ERIKSEN, B. V., 2002, Die Rolle der deutschen Paläolithforschung in der internationalen Diskussion. *Archäologisches Nachrichtenblatt* 8(1).

FISHER, L., 2000, *Land Use and Technology from Magdalenian to Early Mesolihtic in Southern Germany.* Unpublished dissertation, University of Michigan.

FISHER, L., in press, Hunter-Gatherer Mobility and Food-Getting Technologies: Long-Term Change from Final Paleolithic to Mesolithic in Southern Germany. In *Beyond Foraging and Collecting: Evolutionary Change in Hunter-Gatherer Settlement Systems*, edited by J. B. Fitzhugh & J. Habu. Plenum Press: New York.

GAUDZINSKI, S., 2002, Zwischen DNA-Untersuchung und Typologie? Überlegungen zur inhaltlichen Zukunft der Paläolithforschung in Deutschland. *Archäologisches Nachrichtenblatt* 8 (1).

HAHN, J., & OWEN, L. R., 1985, Blade Technology in the Aurignacien and Gravettian of

Geissenklösterle Cave, Southwest Germany. *World Achaeology 17(1)*, p. 61-75.

HAIDLE, M. N., 2002, Ausblick. *Archäologisches Nachrichtenblatt 8* (1).

HAIDLE, M. N., 2002, Paläolithforschung im Spiegel der Medien. *Archäologisches Nachrichtenblatt 8* (1).

HAIDLE, M. N., ZÖLLER, L., SCHÄFER, D., RICHTER, J. & BÖHNER, U., 2002, Auf dem Abstellgleis? Situation und Chancen der Paläolithforschung in Deutschland. Symposium im Rahmen der 43. Jahrestagung der Hugo-Obermaier-Gesellschaft 17. bis 24. 4. 2001 in Halle. Einführung. *Archäologisches Nachrichtenblatt 8* (1).

HARRIS, S. & JOCHIM, M., 1997, Neue mittelsteinzeitliche Untersuchungen im Federseegebiet. *Archäologische Ausgrabungen in Baden-Württemberg* 1996, p. 29-31.

JOCHIM, M. (ed.), 1993, *Henauhof-Nordwest – Ein mittelsteinzeitlicher Lagerplatz am Federsee.* Materialhefte zur Vor- und Frühgeschichte in Baden-Württemberg 19. Stuttgart: Konrad Theiss Verlag.

JOCHIM, M., 2000, Oberflächenprospektion im Pfrunger Ried bei Ostrach, Kreis Sigmaringen und Willhelmsdorf, Kreis Ravensburg. *Archäologische Ausgrabungen in Baden-Württemberg 1999*, p. 25-27.

JOCHIM, M., GLASS, M., FISHER, L. & MCCARTNEY, P., 1998, Mapping the Stone Age: An interim report on the South German Survey Project. In *Aktuelle Forschungen zum Mesolithikum – Current Mesolithic Research,* edited by N. J. Conard & C.-J. Kind. Urgeschichtliche Materialhefte 12. Tübingen: MoVince Verlag, p. 121-131.

KIESELBACH, P., KIND, C.-J., MILLER, A. M. & RICHTER, D. 2000, *Siebenlinden 2. Ein mesolithischer Lagerplatz bei Rottenburg am Neckar, Kreis Tübingen.* Materialhefte zur Archäologie in Baden-Württemberg 51. Stuttgart: Konrad Theiss Verlag.

KIND, C.-J., 2002, Zurück in die Diskussion! Institutionelle Positionierung der deutschen Paläolithforschung. *Archäologisches Nachrichtenblatt 8* (1).

KRISTIANSEN, K., 2001, *Islands of knowledge – research communities and language.* Paper presented in the session on ‚German archaeological theory and practice in its European context' at the 7th Annual Meeting of the European Association of Archaeologists, Esslingen am Neckar, 19.-23. 9.2001.

MILLER, A. M., 1996, *Die Tierknochenfunde aus der mesolithischen Station Rottenburg-Siebenlinden 2 (Rosi 2) und das Problem der holozänen Größenveränderungen beim Reh (Capreolus capreolus).* Unpublished M.A. thesis, Tübingen 1996.

MILLER, A. M., 1998, Die Verteilung der faunistischen Reste in Rottenburg-Siebenlinden 2. In *Aktuelle Forschungen zum Mesolithikum – Current Mesolithic Research,* edited by N. J. Conard & C.-J. Kind. Urgeschichtliche Materialhefte 12. Tübingen: MoVince Verlag, p. 281-292.

NIVEN, L., in press, Patterns of Subsistence during the Aurignacian of the Swabian Jura." In *The Chronology of the Aurignacian and the Transitional Technocomplexes: Dating, Stratigraphies, Cultural Implications,* edited by F. D'Errico & J. Zilhao. Proceedings of UISPP Section 6.

NOONE, J., FISHER, L., GLASS, M., JOCHIM, M. & MCCARTNEY, P., 1997, Eine Frühjahrsprospektion im Federseegebiet. *Archäologische Ausgrabungen in Baden-Württemberg* 1996, p. 32-34.

OWEN, L R., 1984, *Archäologische Forschungen auf Banks Island 1970 - 1975. Teil 1: The Microblades of Umingmak.* Urgeschichtliche Materialhefte 5,1. Tübingen: Archaeologica Venatoria.

OWEN, L R., 1996, *Dictionary of Prehistoric Archeology Prähistorisches Wörterbuch English/ German Deutsch/Englisch.* Tübingen: MoVince Verlag.

OWEN, L. R. & PORR, M. (eds.), 1999, *Ethno-Analogy and the Reconstruction of Prehistoric Artefact Use and Production.* Urgeschichtliche Materialhefte 14. Tübingen: MoVince Verlag.

OWEN, L. R. in prep., *Geschlechterrollen und Arbeitsteilung im Jungpaläolithikum Europas.* Habilitation thesis, University of Tübingen.

OWEN, L. R., & UNRATH, G. (eds.), 1986, *Technical Aspects of Microwear Studies on Stone Tools.* Early Man News 9/10/11.

OWEN, L. R., 1988, *Blade and Microblade Technology. Selected Assemblages from the North American Arctic and the Upper Paleolithic of Southwest Germany.* Oxford: BAR International Series 441.

OWEN, L. R., 1989, Klingen- und Mikroklingentechnologie im Jungpaläolithikum Südwestdeutschlands. *Archäologisches Korrespondenzblatt* 19 (2), p. 103-115.

PASDA, C. 2002, Diskussionsforum, AG-Paläolithikum – Inhalte'. *Archäologisches Nachrichtenblatt* 8(1).

PRINDIVILLE, T. J., 2000, Taphonomie und Archäologie der Pferdereste aus Wallertheim, Fundschicht F (Grabung Conard 1991-1994). *Archäologische Informationen* 23/2, p. 271-275.

SPATZ, H., 2002, Die Einbindung der Paläolithforschung in die deutsche Ur- und Frühgeschichtslandschaft. *Archäologisches Nachrichtenblatt* 8 (1).

STEPHAN, E., 2002, Diskussionsforum, AG-Paläolithikum – Organisation'. *Archäologisches Nachrichtenblatt* 8(1).

TROMNAU, G., 2002, Diskussionsforum ,AG-Paläolithikum – Öffentlichkeit und Museum'. *Archäologisches Nachrichtenblatt* 8 (1).

WEINSTOCK, J., 2000, *Late pleistocene reindeer populations in Western and Central Europe. An osteometrical study*. BioArchaeologica 3. Tübingen: MoVince Verlag.

ZIEGLER, M., 2002, Diskussionsforum, AG-Paläolithikum – Publikationswesen'. *Archäologisches Nachrichtenblatt* 8 (1).

SOUTH MORAVIA AS A MEETING PLACE OF AMERICAN AND CZECH RESEARCHERS

Jiří SVOBODA

Résumé: Le but de cette contribution est de résumer brièvement comment les visites occasionnells et informatives par les chercheurs américains en Moravie du sud se sont transformés en projects internationaux plus systématiques.

Abstract: This contribution aims to review briefly how did the occasional and informative visits by American scholars in South Moravia evolved into more systematic international projects.

Due to its central geographic location in the continent, and to its geomorphological character as a natural corridor, Moravia, the eastern part of the present Czech Republic, played a key role in the Upper Paleolithic paleogeography of Europe, especially during the Gravettian period. At present, the richess and complexity of the archaeological record provides potentials for a fruitful international collaboration.

Some American researchers were, in fact, Czechs: let us remember the anthropologist Aleš Hrdlièka and the Quaternary geologist Jiří G. Kukla. However, the first important Czech-American encounter was the visit of American School of Prehistoric Research to Karel Absolon's excavation at Dolní Vìstonice during the 1920s. Since that time, only signatures and inscriptions in the visitors book at the Dolní Vìstonice Research Center attest to sporadic visits by a number of important American scholars such as Hallam Movius, for example.

Since the 1970s, these visits became more systematic in character and focused on more topical projects. This was the time-period when the basic chronological/environmental framework of the Moravian Upper Paleolithic had principally been completed by the Czech archaeologists and Quaternary geologists. Using this framework, researchers from overseas focused on specific questions, topics and methodologies, and expanded the scope of research into new areas. In fact, some renomed researchers were invited by the Czech colleagues to realise concrete topical analyses that were still lacking at the time.

Alexander Marshack investigated Gravettian and Magdalenian art under the microscope, and the results were incorporated into his synthetic studies, such as *The Roots of Civilization* (Marshack 1992). Since the 80s, Olga Soffer centered more systematically on Gravettian settlement system, with a special emphasis on economies and technologies. Starting with the technology of firing the ceramic figurines, which has world priority for antiquity in the Gravettian of Moravia (Soffer et al. 1993), Soffer discovered possible evidence of another new technology based on perishable materials: traces of earliest textiles and basketery structures, as imprinted in some of the fired clay lumps (Soffer et al. 1998). During her research, Soffer introduced to South Moravia other American specialists in the individual technologies, such as Pamela Vandiver for the ceramics (Vandiver et al. 1989) and Jim Adovasio for the textiles (Adovasio et al. 2001).

Other specific areas of interest include the faunal analysis of Gravettian and Epigravettian sites, as realised by Dixie West (2001), and use-wear analysis, including search for organic residues, realised by Bruce Hardy (1999, see also Tomášková 1994).

Of course, there have been discussions about interpretation of the evidence, but their nature was more empirical than paradigmatic. Applying Binford's sceptical views on the evidence of early human hunting, the old question of Gravettian mammoth hunting versus scavenging has been raised, and the evidence from the mammoth bone deposits has been reconsidered (Soffer 1993). Even if the question still remains unresolved, a positive result of this discussion have been more careful statements about mammoth hunting in the recent literature (e.g., West 2001). Later, the first announcement of textile evidence from the Gravettian (Soffer et al. 1998, etc.) evoked an *a priori* criticism from some Czech archaeologists, who, however, were not Paleolithic specialists and were unsufficiently informed about the state of the evidence. Nevertheless, this polemic stimulated further descriptive and photographic-documentary work on the original textile imprints, and its impact is therefore positive.

An important aspect of the Moravian Upper Paleolithic settlements is their relative complexity, including evidence of structures, technologies, hunting, symbolism, and also the skeletal remains of their inhabitants and producers, the first anatomically modern humans. A small but important sample of the Upper Paleolithic population from Moravia, found in a relatively good state of preservation (e.g. Dolní Vìstonice, Pavlov, Mladeè), has attracted many of the world´s physical anthropologists and doctoral students to obtain a first-hand knowledge of these fossil materials. Whatever ideology the American anthropologists defend regarding the models of modern human origins, several of them studied these materials systematically and widely contributed to their analysis: Milford Wolpoff, Fred Smith, David Frayer, Erik Trinkaus, Trent Holliday and others (cf. Wolpoff 1999). During these researches, the focus moved from morphological description of the cranial remains to a more functional analysis of the postcranial (Sládek et al. 2000, Trinkaus & Jelínek 1997, Trinkaus et al. 2000, etc.). Thus, as in the archaeological line of research, the American approach brought an emphasis on behavior, functions, and adaptation.

Growing interest in and international discussion of the origins of the Upper Paleolithic, together with the somehow underestimated role of Central Europe in this global process, led Czech and American researchers to start a joint field project at the Early Upper Paleolithic site of Stránská skála in 1997-1999. On the American side, this project was formed by Ofer Bar-Yosef, Gilliane Monnier, and Gilbert Tostevin. This international collaboration also made it possible to draw more clearly the comparisons between Moravian and Near Eastern Initial Upper Paleolithic assemblages and to define their specific technologies, such as the Emiro-Bohunician technology, for example. A final monographic volume placing Stránská skála within the context of Early Upper Paleolithic formation processes is currently in preparation.

While in some other countries the differences between European and American theoretical backgrounds may have sometimes led to a confrontation, South Moravia is a place where the the variability in interests, topics and approaches has led to a fruitful international collaboration. The chronological framework, as created by the Czech archaeologists, evoked no dispute from the American side. Inversely, the new aspects and methods introduced from America were welcome, and even if not always accepted unequivocally, (as in the mammoth scavenging scenario, for example), they initiated a revision of models previously taken as certain, with additional analysis and discussion. In sum, the ongoing collaboration is is reflected in the structure of the existing teams and in the rich bibliographies of joint publications.

Academy of Sciences of the Czech Republic
Institute of Archaeology
Paleolithic and Paleoethnology Research Center
69201 Dolní Vìstonice, CZECH REPUBLIC
svoboda@iabrno.cz

BIBLIOGRAPHY

ADOVASIO, J.M., SOFFER, O., HYLAND, D.C., ILLINGSWORTH, J.S., KLÍMA, B., & SVOBODA, J. 2001, Perishable industries from Dolní Vistonice I: New insights into the nature and origin of the Gravettian. *Archaeology, Ethnology and Anthropology of Eurasia* 2 (6), p. 48-65.

HARDY, B. 1999, Preliminary results of residue and use-wear analysis of stone tools from two Mesolithic sites, Northern Bohemia, Czech Republic. *Archeologické rozhledy* 51, p. 274-279.

MARSHACK, A. 1992, *The roots of civilization*, 2nd edition. McGraw-Hill, New York.

SLÁDEK, V., TRINKAUS, E., HILLSON, S.W., & HOLLIDAY, T. 2000: *The people of the Pavlovian. The Dolní Vìstonice Studies vol. 5*, Institute of Archaeology, Brno.

SOFFER, O. 1993, Upper Paleolithic adaptations in Central and Eastern Europe and man-mammoth interactions. In: O.Soffer and N.D.Praslov, eds., *From Kostenki to Clovis*. New York - London: Plenum, p. 31-49.

SOFFER, O., VANDIVER, P., KLÍMA, B., & SVOBODA, J. 1993, The pyrotechnology of performance art: Moravian venuses and wolverines. In: H.Knecht et al., ed., *Before Lascaux*. CRC Press, Boca Raton, Ann Arbor, London, Tokyo, p. 259-275.

SOFFER, O., ADOVASIO, J.M., HYLAND, D.C., KLÍMA, B., & SVOBODA, J. 1998, Perishable technologies and the genesis of the Eastern Gravettian. *Anthropologie* 36, p. 43-68.

TOMÁŠKOVÁ, S., 1994, Use-wear analysis and its spatial interpretation. In *Pavlov I, ERAUL 66/The Dolní Vìstonice Studies vol. 2*, p. 28-40.

TRINKAUS, E., & JELÍNEK, J. 1997, Human remains from the Moravian Gravettian: The Dolní Vìstonice 3 postcrania. *Journal of Human Evolution* 33, p. 33-82.

TRINKAUS, E., SVOBODA, J., WEST, D.L., SLÁDEK, V., HILLSON, S.W., DROZDOVÁ, E., & FIŠÁKOVÁ, M. 2000, Human remains from the Moravian Gravettian: Morphology and taphonomy of isolated elements from the Dolní Vìstonice II site. *Journal of Archaeological Science* 27, p. 1115-1132.

VANDIVER, P., SOFFER, O., KLÍMA, B., & SVOBODA, J. 1989, The origins of ceramic technology at Dolní Vìstonice, Czechoslovakia. *Science* 246, p. 1002-1008.

WEST, D., 2001, Analysis of the fauna recovered from the 1986/1987 excavations at Dolní Vìstonice II, western slope. *Památky archeologické* 92, p. 98-123.

WOLPOFF, M.H. 1999, *Paleoanthropology*, 2nd edition. Boston: McGraw-Hill.

THE HISTORIC AND LEGAL CONTEXT OF FOREIGN ACQUISITIONS OF PALEOLITHIC ARTIFACTS FROM THE PÉRIGORD: 1900 TO 1941

Randall WHITE

Résumé: Au début du XXe siècle les archéologues étrangers étaient très actifs en Périgord. En l'absence des lois contrôlantes, les fouilles et les achats ont eu comme résultat l'exportation de la France des centaines de milliers d'objets archéologiques. Cet article, en utilisant quelques exemples détaillés, cherche à comprendre le contexte légal, politique, scientifique et interpersonnel de cette activité étrangère plutôt destructrice.

Abstract: The early part of the twentieth century saw intense excavation and collecting activity in the Périgord by American and other foreign archaeologists. In the absence of controlling legislation, this activity resulted in the departure from France of hundreds of thousands of Paleolithic artifacts. The present article seeks to explore, using a few detailed examples, the complex legal, political, scientific and inter-personal context in which this rather destructive foreign activity occurred.

INTRODUCTION

The Dordogne region of SW France has been a focus of attention of prehistoric researchers from around the world since the 1860s, when Lartet and Christy's pioneering research brought to light a rich and complicated Middle and Upper Paleolithic record. As early as the 1860s, American researchers and museum representatives were active in the region, but the American presence was at its most intense in the first three decades of the twentieth century. During this period, America was in a period of good economic times in which the country was expanding its intellectual and scientific horizons. Most American museums made major acquisitions.

The affluence in America coincided with a situation in which Western Europe, and perhaps post- World War I France in particular, were in economic "straights." The money offered by foreign museum representatives for a few dusty artifacts undoubtedly represented a tantalizing opportunity for a measure of financial security in very insecure times. In this context, American museums profited by filling their reserves with tens of thousands of artifacts. The result was that well over 150,000 French Paleolithic artifacts found their way into American museum displays & drawers. Most of these legally-obtained objects, comprised of lithic tools, bone/antler implements, personal ornaments and art objects, were acquired by The Peabody Museum at Yale University, The Peabody Museum at Harvard University, The

Smithsonian Institution in Washington, The Field Museum of Natural History in Chicago, the American Museum of Natural History in New York and the National Museum of Canada in Ottawa. The effect was also felt outside of prehistoric archaeology. It was during this period, for example, that New York's Metropolitan Museum obtained its enormous French Medieval collections, including entire churches, dismantled and transported to Manhattan.

OTHER FOREIGNERS

Americans were not the only foreigners with an intense interest in the Paleolithic record of the Dordogne. Late nineteenth century German nationalism and expansionism had as consequences, intense research and collecting activities. In the Dordogne, this took the form of large-scale research and collecting activities undertaken by Otto Hauser, the Swiss archaeologist and antiquities dealer, who was the bête noire of French prehistorians in SW France.

Most European prehistorians are familiar with the official French version of the *«affaire Hauser,»* according to which Hauser's expulsion from France and the seizure of his property was justified by his status as an antiquities dealer who destroyed

Paleolithic sites in order to sell the artifacts recovered. The real story is only now coming to light as a result of the analysis of French and German archives related to Hauser's professional activities and his relations with French archaeologists. In what follows, it is important to keep in mind that Hauser, a Swiss national, was subject to precisely the same legal and administrative structure as were the Americans. However, the outcome for him was dramatically different.

The Hauser affair lingered for 30 years, ending with his death in 1932, and influenced in a number of ways- both positive and negative- the ability of Americans to conduct research and obtain museum collections. His activities in the Dordogne began in 1898, less than three decades after the Franco-Prussian War, and ended with his flight from France in 1914, at the outbreak of World War I. However, his departure resolved almost nothing. His land holdings and some yet-to-be-exported collections were placed under sequester, as was done with the property of all foreign nationals from belligerent countries (even though Hauser was a Swiss citizen). Peyrony was named supervisor of the sequestration. However, archaeologically-speaking, Hauser had done nothing more illegal than other foreigners had. Therefore, no permanent action could be taken with respect to his property, unless it could be shown that he collaborated with the enemies of France.

Unlike the Americans, Hauser was a real presence on French soil. He took out leases on numerous sites and purchased others (Hauser 1911). He excavated many key Paleolithic sites, some of them with surprising care (see Hauser 1916) and others with an eye to the sale of collections to German museums. He also organized scientific visits by groups of German scientists and museum directors. If American workers in the Hauser period were tolerated and largely invulnerable to limits on their activities, Hauser's German affiliations, his close relationship with anti-clerics such as the de Mortillets, and his ambitious excavation activities made him a target. Accusations of espionage emerged in Les Eyzies as early as 1906. In spite of all this, Hauser maintained a cordial, even friendly relationship with Peyrony until serious personal conflicts drove a wedge between them in 1907. Up to that point, Peyrony actually sold artifacts to Hauser and, incredibly, nominated him for entry into the Masonic Lodge. He also defended him against allegations that he was a spy. However, beginning in 1907, Peyrony seems to have declared war on

Otto Hauser, ultimately ressurecting charges of espionage on the eve of World War I.

LEGAL ISSUES

Peyrony raised the alarm with the *Ministère de l'Instruction Publique et Beaux-Arts*, who supported him in his efforts to restrict the activities of foreign archaeologists. In 1908 an attempt was made to pass a law that would give the state control over archaeological excavations and submit excavation projects to review by competent authorities. The projected law, published in the *Bulletin de la Société Préhistorique Française*, provoked a cry of protest from the *Société's* membership, then dominated by enlightened amateurs. The legislation was defeated largely because the *Société* took a formal position against it. Had this legislation succeeded, the Hauser affair would never have occurred and it is unlikely that American institutions would have succeeded in excavating and exporting collections. Given the failure of this law and hence the absence of controlling legislation, the Ministère de l'Instruction Publique et Beaux Arts, represented in the Dordogne by Peyrony, set out to lease as many sites as possible to keep them out of the hands of the foreign menace.

It has never been an easy matter for foreigners to undertake research activities on French soil. Today, laws and procedures are firmly in place to regulate their research activities. Until 1941, however, there were no laws, apart from ministerial classification of archaeological sites as «*monuments historiques,*» that prevented excavation of sites and the exportation of resulting collections. Legally, the archaeological record was (and remains today) the private property of the site owner. All that was required on the part of archaeologists, whether they were foreigners or French citizens, was permission of the owner, usually in the form of a lease taken on the property concerned. The law of December 31, 1913, ultimately afforded a small measure of control over sites that were classified as «*monuments historiques*», a fact that led to a flurry of classification orders in the 1920s.

Foreigners wishing to excavate in France or to obtain collections, needed merely to maintain good relations with the small number of existing archaeological authorities, who, in any event, had no legal power to control their activities. This allowed foreign institutions a free hand to fill their museum drawers. Ironically, it was the Vichy regime that acted to change this situation by passing the law of 1941, which was later affirmed by the post-war government. This law gave the French State control over excavation and exportation of archaeological collections, while leaving proprietary rights to the site owner.

CONCEPTUAL AND STRUCTURAL MATTERS

The worldwide dispersal of French cultural heritage resulted not simply from an absence of legal control. In the early twentieth century, archaeology, and especially European Paleolithic archaeology, had a very different view of the archaeological record. It was generally viewed with a geologist's eye, the concern being more with typological evolution than with human behavior (Sackett 1968). According to this conceptual framework, only a representative sample of unique and chronologically diagnostic artifacts needed to be retained. So-called «duplicates» were considered expendable and were often dispersed to other museums or left in the backdirt.

French prehistory in the early twentieth century was not professionalized. Many of the well-known excavators were interested amateurs. At the same time, government funds for the excavation and preservation of sites were exceedingly rare, and virtually unavailable to non-professionals. This placed both the excavators and museums in a compromised position. Unless independently wealthy, amateurs were obliged to sell parts of their collections to finance future work. With very limited funds available, French museums were forced to purchase the French patrimony from private owners. Under these conditions, some severe choices had to be made, often resulting in the breaking up of collections. Often, the portions not purchased by French museums were sold to private collectors or museums abroad.

SOME CONSEQUENCES OF THE ABSENCE OF CONTROLLING LEGISLATION

In this context, it was relatively easy for American prehistorians and private collectors to operate in France. The acquisition of important prehistoric collections began in the 1860s and continued up to World War II. While available archives indicate a certain number of efforts by French prehistorians, such as Denis Peyrony, Louis Capitan, Henri Breuil and Louis Didon, to limit or prevent American activities, their powers were restricted to classifying as «*monuments historiques*» the most important of the sites concerned and to working behind the scenes to prevent leases by American archaeologists. Of course, since these same archaeologists were financially involved with the Americans, their situation was at best ambiguous. There was avarice involved on both sides. American institutions were buying Paleolithic material beyond all reasonable teaching needs. At the same time, Breuil, Capitan, Peyrony, Bouyssonie, Didon and a number of site owners and amateurs gained financially from the sale of artifacts, and from their advice to Americans as to who had the best collections and how much money should be offered.

Peyrony's frenetic pace of excavation before World War I was motivated in large part by his desire to prevent Hauser from excavating important sites. In 1910, upon hearing from Marcel Castanet of Hauser's interest in excavating the newly discovered Abri Castanet, Peyrony took out a twenty-year lease on the site and had Castanet excavate it on his behalf. Peyrony signed more than a dozen additional leases in the period leading up to World War I.

During Hauser's actual presence in SW France, his specter was frequently beneficial to Americans, since Peyrony preferring to have Americans excavating and collecting rather than leaving such activities to the ever-present Hauser, who was buying, leasing and excavating sites at an alarming rate. For example, in 1912, George Grant MacCurdy, then at Yale University, arrived in Les Eyzies and had some free time on his hands. Peyrony proposed to him that he excavate the cave of La Combe, a site that Peyrony himself had tested some years previously. MacCurdy (1914a: 157) described the situation thus

During the summer of 1912, after having completed a tour of the paleolithic caves of France and Spain, I found myself in the picturesque little village of Les Eyzies with a desire to know more about troglodite culture and two or three weeks still at my disposal. I had always wanted to explore a Quaternary cave. Knowing this, Peyrony came to my rescue. Some five years previously he had made a sounding near the entrance of the small cave of La Combe (Dordogne) about one hour's walk to the south of Les Eyzies, and had found enough in the way of flint chips and bones to warrant future research. Moreover within the cave Peyrony, Peyrille, and young Casimir Mercier, son of the proprietor, had each found several specimens, including a bone point with cleft base, several perforated shells, and a polishing stone. The perforated shells and polishing stone later came into possession of Professor Max Verworn of Bonn, Germany; while I obtained through purchase from Peyrony and Mercier the bone point and a few flint implements.

I obtained a lease of the cave, and with two workmen, Marcelin Berniche and Casimir Mercier, began excavations on August 5th.

MacCurdy excavated for a period of a few days and the important Châtelperronian, Aurignacian and Mousterian collections were exported without difficulty to the United States.

It was also at this time that MacCurdy, collaborating with Henry Fairfield Osborn and Nels Nelson of the American Museum of Natural History, purchased from Louis Didon remarkable Gravettian and Aurignacian collections from the newly excavated sites of Abri Labattut and Abri Blanchard.(MacCurdy 1914b; Simek 1986). This policy of blocking Hauser at all costs created a kind of double standard that allowed Americans throughout the Hauser period to obtain and export archaeological collections with impunity, while Hauser was vilified for doing the same things.

The espionage accusations against Hauser were clearly false (Delluc and Delluc 1999), but they show the hatred that existed between Peyrony & him and the extreme measures necessitated by the absence of controlling legislation. This state of hostility remained in the years preceding World War I. Hauser continued to excavate, to export collections and to associate with German scientists and institutions. Hauser, fearing for his life, fled France forever in 1914, leaving his substantial collections in the hands of his local collaborator and excavator Jean Leyssales. Thereafter, it did not take long for the accusations of espionage to be resurrected against him by Denis Peyrony and his collaborators in order to justify the permanent seizure of the real estate and archaeological collections concerned.

These collections and other holdings were immediately placed under sequester. After the end of hostilities, Hauser and Leyssales moved to have the sequester lifted by the court in Bordeaux. The motion was rejected on the grounds that Hauser and Leyssales had represented institutions of an enemy state. The French State successfully sought to enforce its *droit de préemption* and Hauser's property was put up for public auction. Peyrony was charged by the state with the responsibility of bidding at auction for real estate considered to be of archaeological importance. He was also charged with the responsibility of recovering for the *Musée National de Préhistoire* any remaining artifact collections in the possession of Leyssales.

Peyrony was able to force an inventory of the Hauser collections, but strongly suspected that much was being hidden from him. The legal machinations surrounding Hauser's property would continue until 1931 and the specter of Hauser impacted the subsequent reaction of French authorities and prehistorians to the ever-increasing research and collecting activities of Americans.

After Hauser's departure, with the immediate threat dissipated, there was more resistance to the American presence, except in cases where personal friendships developed between American workers and French authorities. For example, Breuil's friendship with Henry Field allowed the latter to export about 30,000 artifacts to the Field Museum of Natural History in the late 1920's (Field 1955). Largely in response to intensive American activity, a systematic effort was undertaken between 1921 and 1929 to classify as many sites as possible as *«monuments historiques.»* Given such status, no excavation, construction or other alterations could take place without the explicit agreement of the minister responsible.

In 1924-27, George Collie and Alonzo Pond, representatives of the Logan Museum of Anthropology at Beloit College, seeking to acquire collections (see White 1992a for the full inventory) for the museum by excavation and purchase, stumbled quite unwittingly into the lingering Hauser and Leyssales affair. They also became involved directly in this new effort to prevent foreign work through the classification of sites. They purchased for 25,000 francs ($1250) a large collection from Leyssales. Leyssales did not tell them that the collection was contested by Peyrony. Before they could transport it back to the US, Peyrony intervened, requiring Pond to cede to the Museum certain parts of the collection that could be identified as belonging to Hauser.

In August 1924, Alonzo Pond, on a serious buying trip (see for example, White and Dobres 1992; Matthews 1991, 1992; White and Roussot 1992a) visited Louis Didon, the excavator of Abri Blanchard at Sergeac (Didon 1911, 1912a, 1912b; Pond 1925; White 1992b). Presuming that Didon would not sell the Blanchard beads, Pond queried him concerning the legitimacy and value of another collection of beads. In the course of his discussions with Didon, Pond apparently revealed the amount of his offer for the other beads. Didon responded with, «well, if that's the kind of money you're talking, why don't you buy my Blanchard necklace (A. Pond, personal communication)»? A letter from Pond to Frank Logan dated August 12, 1924, indicates that he had elicited a selling price of 15,000 francs ($750) from Didon. It is no small matter that Didon was one of Hauser's most bitter enemies, accusing him of being nothing more than an artifact merchant.

In 1926 they arranged with Denis Peyrony to make «donations» to L. Capitan (7,000 francs or $350) and to the Ministère de l'Instruction Publique et Beaux-Arts («pour la Caisse des recherches des Monuments historiques») (3,000 francs or $150) in order to procure large collections from La Ferrassie and La Madeleine. These amounts were paid in January 1926, accompanied by letters copied from handwritten drafts sent by Peyrony (letter from Collie to Pond, January 6, 1926) for just this purpose. In return for these donations to aid future excavations, Collie stated that,

Si l'Etat pouvait disposer en faveur de notre musée d'une série d'objéts constitituée par les nombreux doubles du Musée des Eyzies, provenant du gisement de la Madeleine, j'en serais très heureux et reconnaissant.

In the letter to Capitan, Collie's (actually Peyrony's) wording was slightly different:

Je serais très heureux si vous vouliez bien disposer en faveur de notre musée d'une série d'objets constituée par les nombreux doubles déposés dans les magasins archéologiques du Musée des Eyzies-de-Tayac.

The collections from La Madeleine and La Ferrassie, taken from the drawers of the Musée des Eyzies, were received at the Logan Museum in two shipments, one in March, 1926 and the other in June, 1926.

Pond and Collie returned to Les Eyzies in August 1926, to begin excavations at Rocher de la Peine (Ehrhardt 1991; 1992; Ehrhardt, Roussot and White 1992). They decided to collaborate with Peyrony because,

This seems advisable as a secret ring of men is believed to exist here who are getting all the valuable material they can get by hook or crook and sending it for a big price to Germany. Unfortunately, Esclafer, the peasant who leased us the Rocher de la Peine is believed to be a member of the ring and that apparently has made Peyrony suspicious that we were in league with him. We have told Peyrony that we were on the square and that we would advise with him and work with him as long as we are here. This has placated him and he evidently feels better about our being here. So we plan to carry out his wishes in all respects.

During the Rocher de la Peine excavations, the workman Merlan showed Pond and Collie the excavations that he had been undertaking at the site of La Ruth {sic}(Abri Cellier) near Le Moustier. Collie negotiated rights to excavate at La Ruth when the Rocher de la Peine excavations were completed. These negotiations included the signing of a lease with the proprietor of the site, Madame Baptiste Cellier. In anticipation of these excavations, Collie purchased from Madame Cellier, the enormous collection of Aurignacian artifacts already excavated from the site by Fernand Merlan (Nesbitt 1928; Peyrony 1926, 1946; White and Knecht 1992).

In the same letter, Collie notes that Louis Didon, the great enemy of Hauser, had agreed to lease them the Abri Labattut,

...the lease to be indefinite and to include all the material taken out recently. The whole to cost 55,000 francs. I felt that we ought to take the offer largely because the cave has a Solutrean level in it and we sorely need Solutrean material, it is almost impossible to buy it or find it. Now we have a site which though difficult to dig promises much in the way of results. We hope to close the bargain on the 5th and to have the material packed and forwarded at once.

The price, which was actually 54,250 francs (about $2,700), included the purchase of Didon's enormous ethnographic collection (letter from Collie to Logan, October 10, 1926), consisting of 560 objects, primarily from Africa and Oceania. According to Pond (letter to Collie, November 24, 1925),

Didon also says that he will have to sell his ethnographical collection this year as the tax on collections is more than he can stand.

Part of this collection, much of which remains at the Logan Museum, comes from the earliest French expeditions to the South Pacific, led by the great French explorer Jean François de la Pérouse.

At about the same time, Pond followed up on earlier advice from Count Bégouën to approach Léo Bélanger, the proprietor of the Magdalenian open-air site of Limeuil, concerning the possible purchase of engraved limestone plaquettes from this site (Capitan and Bouyssonie 1924). Bélanger informed Pond that Jean Bouyssonie, with whom Louis Capitan had excavated the site, had the plaquettes at his school near Brive and was acting as agent for the sale of the engravings (letter from Pond to George Collie, August 11, 1924; letter from Jean Bouyssonie to Léo Bélanger, August 25, 1924). Arrangements were made for Pond to visit Bouyssonie in order to view the plaquettes. As a result, Bouyssonie intervened to facilitate the purchase of 40 of these plaquettes as well as a significant number of stone and bone tools for a price of 15,000 francs ($750), much higher than the 7,000 franc asking price earlier indicated by Henri Bégouen. The 15,000 francs was paid directly to Bouyssonie who deducted his 10% commission before forwarding the remainder to Bélanger (letter from Jean Bouyssonie to Léo Bélanger, October 7, 1924). Beloit's collection constitutes the largest single

Figure 1 : George Collie (left) and Denis Peyrony in 1927 at Le Moustier
(Beloit College Archives, with permission)

collection of Limeuil engravings apart from those at the *Musée des Antiquités Nationales* and the *Musée National de Préhistoire* (Tosello 1997) and is critical to a full analysis of this important site.

The collections tax imposed in 1925 stimulated many collectors to sell collections that may have otherwise ended up in French museums. This was Didon's motive for selling his magnificent ethnographic collection. Pond, in a letter to Collie dated November 24, 1925, stated that,

If it is at all possible for us to raise funds we can undoubtedly make some mighty good purchases next summer as that new tax law will hit a lot of them hard.

Severe problems arose with Peyrony over the 1927 Beloit excavations at Abri Cellier (White 1992a). The sequence of events is best described in Collie's own words (letter from Collie to Logan, September 26, 1926):

That same day (September 20, 1926) we talked over preliminaries with the peasant owner of leasing not buying La Ruth, taking over the flints already excavated, a splendid lot of them, numbering about 4,000. All this for 35,000 francs, the lease running 15 years. Before we finally could get the lease papers made out, Peyrony scenting what was going on obtained from Paris an order to classify La Ruth and to put it under state control. So we were euchred out of the lease. Pond and I got our heads together, telegraphed to some of our archaeological friends as to their opinion of the fairness of such a move on Peyrony's part, when we had a good claim to the diggings. Finally we decided to go to Paris post haste to see the American Ambassador. We went Thursday and secured an interview with the 2nd Secretary on Friday and laid our case before him. He promised to acquaint the French govt. with our views and was quite hopeful he would be able to secure the lease for us, but it would probably take a month or more to get the matter settled.

Collie's observations are confirmed in Peyrony's personal journal. Peyrony notes on September 17, 1926, that he had sent a report on that day to the *Ministère de l'Instruction Publique et Beaux-Arts* seeking the classification of Abri Cellier as a *"monument historique"*. This matter was apparently treated with some urgency, as Peyrony already notes on September 22, that he had received notification that the procedures for classifying the site had been begun.

On October 3, Collie wrote the following to Frank Logan:

Though we were forbidden to work at La Ruth, Pond and I decided to take the bull by the horns and buy all that has been taken from that site thus far, even though the government has stopped our working there. So we went to the peasant who owns the place Madame Cellier and asked her what she would take for the 4,000 pieces that she had on hand and she replied 18,000 francs for the collection and I will sign a lease for the site for 15 years, which you may pay 18,000 francs for provided the government removes the ban, so we had the papers made out, receipt and lease, which she signed with a cross as she can not write, thus we have a very fine Aurignacian collection and the first claim on the rich site of La Ruth.

Collie spent most of the winter of 1926-27 in Les Eyzies waiting for final authorization to excavate at La Ruth. Peyrony was clearly working to prevent the excavation. Peyrony knew how important the site was and wished to preserve it. Collie's problems also arose from the fact that the American Embassy was apparently not using the full force of its offices. Finally, on April 27, 1927 and at Collie's request, the President of Beloit College wrote to the President of the United States, Calvin Coolidge, asking him to intervene with the State Department to compel them to force the hand of the French authorities. On May 20, after 8 months of waiting, formal permission to excavate was granted, subject to certain conditions imposed by Peyrony (White and Knecht 1992). In the meantime, Peyrony had succeeded in having the site classified as a *"monument historique."*

In a letter to the Director of the Beaux-Arts dated November 29, 1926, Peyrony indicates his concern over the "La Ruth" excavations and the problems being created by American money:

{American universities} étant fort riches, leurs représentants offrent pour les terrains contenant des gisements des sommes d'autant plus élevées qu'elles sont encore favorisées par le change. Des dépôts loués 1000 f. avant guerre arrivent au prix fabuleux de 20 à 25,000 f., prix qu'il ne nous est pas possible d'atteindre. C'est ainsi que le gisement de l'abri Cellier, au Ruth, qui est en instance de classement, a été loué par le Collège Beloit une somme fort élevée.

Cette manière de procéder nous enlève non seulement nos richesses scientifiques, mais entame

notre considération et nous crée des difficultés avec les propriétaires qui ne veulent plus nous louer, attendant «l'Américain.»

D'un autre côté, le sieur Otto Hauser, ce marchand qui bouleversait nos gisements avant guerre, reparait en la personne de son associé Leyssale Ce dernier fouille, ou fait fouiller clandestinement et expédie en Allemagne le produit de ses recherches. C'est ainsi que ce qui avait été découvert à l'abri Cellier avant l'instance de classement a été envoyé à Hauser et vendu comme «aurignacien sans provenance.» C'est donc la déstruction en grand de notre patrimoine préhistorique qui recommence comme avant guerre. Ce ne sera bientôt plus qu'une vaste exploitation si le gouvernement ne prend pas les mésures nécessaires et rapides qui s'imposent. A mon humble avis, deux solutions s'imposent:

1. Faire déclarer par une lois tous les dépôts richesses nationales, comme cela existe en Tchécoslovaquie, en Russie, etc. - Autoriser les fouilles, mais les produits restent la propriété de l'Etat, comme en Espagne. Toute expédition d'antiquités non accompagnée d'un permis de circulation devrait être arrêtée à la douane

2. Autoriser les fouilles en les surveillant et en réservant pour les musées nationaux les squelettes humains, les oeuvres d'art, les pièces rares et des séries complètes d'objets découverts dans chaque gisement. Toute personne agissant dans un but pécuniaire devrait être empêchée de fouiller.

There is more than a little disingenuousness on Peyrony's part, since he and Capitan had already sold collections from La Ferrassie and La Madeleine to Beloit. Indeed, as early as 1901, Peyrony and his Hauser-fighting colleagues had been involved in the sale of prehistoric collections to American and even German museum representatives.

In considering the La Ferrassie-La Madeleine sale, Capitan had advised Peyrony (letter, Capitan to Peyrony, January 8, 1925):

«Pour le petit Pound {sic} très bien mais tenez le garde et méfiez-vous de lui. Je l'ai vu à Strasbourg Il ne m'a pas paru bien instruit mais commerçant à coups de dollar. En tout cas pour éviter tout ennui, il faudrait aviser Verdier et ne rien faire sans son assentiment. Il ne faudrait pas que Pound {sic} bavardant cela nous retombe sur le nez.»

It seems clear from this and other correspondence, that Peyrony was discretely involved in precisely the kind of pecuniary activity that his proposed legislation sought to stem.

MacCurdy was extremely active in the Périgord in the 1920s. He purchased some remarkable objects, notably from Grotte Rey, Les Combarelles and La Mouthe, at the 1921 public auction of Emile Rivière's collections. After holding the summer excavations of the *American School of Prehistoric Research* at La Quina in the Charente between 1921-1923, MacCurdy moved his operations to the Mousterian and Gravettian site of Abri des Merveilles, at Sergeac in the Vézère Valley. He excavated there from 1924 to 1930 (MacCurdy 1931), and with the exception of a few representative and unusual objects, the several thousand artifacts from the site were exported without difficulty to the United States. The majority of these are housed at the National Museum of Natural History (Smithsonian) in Washington.

On a different front, Henri Breuil, also (with Peyrony, Capitan and Didon) a devoted enemy of Otto Hauser, had developed a close friendship with Henry Field, a curator at the Field Museum of Natural History in Chicago. Field had been charged by the Field Museum with the responsibility of mounting a new Hall of Man. To this end, he was granted a significant budget for the acquisition of European Paleolithic collections. Field and Breuil made several trips together in SW France and Northern Spain, the expenses being covered by the Field Museum. Breuil's role (Field 1955) was to target available private collections for Field (for example, see Romanowicz 1991; de Beaune, Roussot and White 1989 and Perry 1993) and to act as intermediary in their acquisition. The result was the expenditure of 100,986F (about $5,000) (not including the acquisition of the Cap-Blanc skeleton) to purchase tens of thousands of objects, including hundreds of bone/antler artifacts and works of art. With the exception of the famous churinga from La Roche de Lalinde, all of these were exported to the United States. Périgord collections included in these purchases include:Grotte des Eyzies, Abri Mège, Grotte de la Mairie, Grotte des Grèzes. La Souquette, Abri Blanchard, Abri Labattut, Laugerie-Basse, Abri Brouillard (Tabaterie), Cap-Blanc, Combe-Capelle, Font-de-Gaume, Fourneau-du-Diable, Gorge d'Enfer, La Croze de Tayac, La Ferrassie, La Madeleine, La Micoque, La Mouthe, La Roche de Lalinde, Laugerie-Haute, Laussel, Le Moustier, Abri Cellier, La Rochette, Font-Brunel, La Faurelie 1, Raymonden-Chancelade, and La Tuilière.This buying binge ended in 1929 (to the great disappointment of Henry Field), when the Director of the Field Museum decided that additional artifacts were not needed.

Yet another foreign excavator and collector in the 1920s was H-M Ami of the Nationl Museum of Canada (White 1980, 1986, 1988; White and Welté 1992). Ami, a close friend of Peyrony, excavated for several years at Combe-Capelle-Bas, recovering and exporting to Canada thousands of Mousterian objects. At the same time, he undertook the sieving of Peyrony's backdirt at La Ferrassie and Laugerie-Haute, recovering and exporting roughly 15,000 tools. These collections are a testimony to what Peyrony threw away. In addition, Ami purchased and exported thousands of objects, primarily lithic tools, from dozens of sites in the Dordogne.

Ami's collecting activities in the Périgord were massive (more than 50,000 objects) and the collections exported to Canada contain materials (sometimes hundreds, even thousands of objects) from the following sites:

Fourneau-du-Diable, Rebières, Tourtoirac, Oreille d'Enfer, Chez-Galou, Laugerie-Basse, Laugerie-Haute, La Ferrassie, La Mouthe, Rocher de la Peine, Cro-le-Biscot, Cap-Blanc, Laussel, Grotte des Eyzies, Château des Eyzies, Abri Pataud, Cro-Magnon, La Madeleine, Reignac, Fongal, Abri Blanchard, Abri Castanet, Abri Pagès, Abri Cellier, Le Moustier, Longueroche, La Forge, Grotte de la Grèze, La Micoque, Plâteau de Marquay, Grotte Vidal, Plâteau de Peyzac, Plâteau de l'Espinasse, Combe-Capelle-Bas, Roc de Combe-Capelle, Terme-Pialat, Abri de Soucy, Combe Grenal, Pech de la Boissière, Jean-Blanc, Gour de l'Arche, Petit Puyrousseau, Badegoule, Le Four de Laussel, and Solvieux. His death in 1931 put an end to these activities. Remarkably, Peyrony's monograph on Laugerie-Haute is dedicated to Ami's memory.

The Great Depression resulted in financial problems for American museums. At Beloit, Frank Logan no longer had the ability to finance such expeditions. By the late 1920s, some doors began to close for American excavators in the Dordogne. In the early

Figure 2 : The 1925 trench into the talus at the Abri des Merveilles. George Grant MacCurdy is visible in the distance as is the wall of the abri (Castanet family archives, with permission).

1930s, MacCurdy sought to excavate the Solutrean site of Pech de la Boissière near Sarlat. Peyrony intervened, classifying the site, obtaining a lease from the site owner and handing the responsibility for excavation to his son Elie. MacCurdy would never again excavate in France.

Nevertheless, from 1930-36, Homer Kidder of Harvard undertook excavations at Roc St. Cirq near Les Eyzies (E. Peyrony and de Sonneville-Bordes 1959) and later at Puy de Lacan in the Corrèze (H. and L. Kidder 1936). As previously, the resulting collections, representing several thousand artifacts, were exported without difficulty, in this case to the Peabody Museum at Harvard University. A final isolated acquisition came about in 1937, when the plaquette engraved with a bear from the Grotte des Eyzies (Breuil 1936-37; White and Roussot 1992b) was donated by Miss Martha White to Beloit College. She had purchased it for 1000 francs from its excavator, Clément Labrousse, a local antiquities dealer in Les Eyzies. A letter of authenticity from, of all people, Denis Peyrony, accompanied it.

The final outcome of American purchases and excavations was not particularly positive. Dispersal of archaeological collections is always destructive. Excavated sites were seldom adequately analyzed or published. Purchased materials were removed from the milieu of French Paleolithic research for decades. We can take some satisfaction from the fact that, for the most part, the important parts of the collections remain intact, and in museum contexts. There is also consolation in the fact that the purchases took many important objects out of private hands- objects that might otherwise have been further dispersed or even discarded.

CONCLUSION

In light of the ease with which Americans were able to excavate and purchase Paleolithic collections, it is difficult to see the anti-Hauser efforts of Peyrony, Breuil, Capitan and Didon as resulting from a commitment to preserve the cultural heritage. It can justifiably be argued that the sum total of destruction and dispersal engendered by American activities exceed by far the damage done by Hauser. A number of factors explain this double standard.

A first explanation lies in the anti-German sentiments so pervasive before and after World War I. In addition,

Hauser's personality and lack of diplomacy did nothing to help his cause. Moreover he was a direct competitor of Peyrony's with respect to the creation of a prehistory museum in Les Eyzies; none of the Americans was sufficiently integrated into the local community to have such ambitions.

We cannot ignore the fact that American money passed from various museum representatives to, among others, Peyrony, Breuil, Capitan and Didon. Hauser acted independently and his activities were in no way lucrative for these individuals, although they created considerable wealth for the local community.

There was also the issue of the personal and professional enmity that existed between Hauser and Peyrony. Hauser and his allies had accused Peyrony of theft and of selling collections and the French responded in kind. Underlying, this enmity lurked Hauser's close personal and professional relationship with the anti-clerics Gabriel and Adrien de Mortillet, venomous adversaries of Breuil, Peyrony and their collaborators.

It is actually frightening to see the degree to which all of this professional and personal hostility, in the absence of controlling legislation, could have such dramatic and catastrophic consequences. For any prehistorian, no matter what the quality of his work, to be forced to flee for fear of his life and to have his property seized and sold at auction by his professional adversaries, would be nothing short of astonishing outside the context of German nationalism and French hatred of the Germans in the early part of the century. In the twenty-first century it is difficult to appreciate the gravity of the situation and the depth of the pre-war and wartime hatred that existed. One thing is clear however; the same sentiments were not directed at American researchers and museum representatives.

The law of September 27, 1941 (validated by the post-War government on September 13, 1945) changed everything. By requiring state-issued excavation permits and interdicting the exportation of collections, it profoundly changed the relationship of foreign prehistorians with their French colleagues. As we have seen, this relationship had often been one of hostility and suspicion. On the American side it had been largely a relationship of exploitation and on the French side one of suspicion and xenophobia. In post-World War II France, if foreign archaeologists were to work in France they had to do so in collaboration with their French hosts. The law gave the French government control of its own archaeological record and required in practice that foreigners conform to acceptable standards of French archaeological research. Of course it also required that the fruits of archaeological excavation remain in France.

This new collaborative spirit is nowhere better exemplified than in the 1950s work of Hallam Movius (MacCurdy's student) of Harvard at La Colombière (Ain) and especially at Abri Pataud (Dordogne). Both of these were collaborative Franco-American projects that have had an important impact on scientific understanding of the past. This work has been widely published in both French and English and the collections remained in France. Far from engendering suspicion and xenophobia, this first-class scientific work and collaborative approach has helped subsequently to create a spirit of trust and common goals...as it should be.

Department of Anthropology
New York University
25 Waverly Place
New York, NY 10003, USA
randall.white@nyu.edu

BIBLIOGRAPHY

ARCHIVES CONSULTED: American Museum of Natural History, New York, NY; Logan Museum of Anthropology, Beloit, WI; Field Museum of Natural History, Chicago, IL; Peabody Museum, Yale University, New Haven, CT; Smithsonian Institution, Washington, DC; National Museum of Canada, Ottawa; Peabody Museum, Harvard University, Cambridge, MA; Musée National de Préhistoire, Les Eyzies, Dordogne; as well as numerous private archives.

BREUIL, H., 1936-37, De quelques oeuvres d'art magdaléniennes inédites ou peu connues,. *Ipek,* 11: p. 1-16.

CAPITAN, L. AND BOUYSSONIE, J., 1924, *Limeuil: son gisement à gravures sur pierres de l'Age du Renne*, Paris: Nourry.

COLLIE, G., 1927, *The Aurignacians and their Culture*. Beloit, Wisconsin:Logan Museum Bulletin I (1).

DE BEAUNE, S., ROUSSOT, A. AND WHITE, R., 1989, Une lampe paléolithique retrouvée dans les collections du Field Museum of Natural History, Chicago. *Bulletin de la Société Préhistorique Ariégoise.* 43: 149-160.

DELLUC, B. AND G., 1981, La dispersion des objets de l'abri Blanchard, *Société d'Etudes et de Recherches des Eyzies.* 30: p. 1-19.

DELLUC, B. AND G., 1999, L'archéologue Otto Hauser à la lumière de quelques documents périgordins. *Bulletin de la Société Historique et Archéologique du Périgord,* CXXVI: p. 705-748.

DIDON, L., 1911, L'Abri Blanchard des Roches (commune de Sergeac). gisement aurignacien moyen, *Bulletin de la Société Historique et Archéologique du Périgord,* 87: p. 246-261 and p. 321-345.

DIDON, L., 1912a, Faits nouveaux constatés dans une station aurignacienne, l'abri Blanchard des Roches près de Sergeac, *L'Anthropologie.* 23: p. 603.

DIDON, L., 1912b, Faits nouveaux constatés dans une station aurignacienne des environs de Sergeac, *Congrès International d'Anthropologie et Archéologie Préhistorique.* 6: p. 337-350.

EHRHARDT, K., 1991, *Rocher de la Peine, commune des Eyzies (Dordogne), France: A historical and archaeological analysis.* Masters thesis, Department of Anthropology, New York University.

EHRHARDT, K., 1992, The bone, antler and ivory assemblage from Rocher de la Peine, commune des Eyzies (Dordogne), *French Paleolithic Collections in the Logan Museum of Anthropology, Beloit College*, R. White and L. Breitborde (eds.), Beloit, Wisconsin, *Bulletin of the Logan Museum of Anthropology, New Series,* 1(2), 203-244.

EHRHARDT, K., ROUSSOT, A. AND WHITE, R., 1992, An engraved cervid from Rocher de la Peine, commune des Eyzies (Dordogne). *French Paleolithic Collections in the Logan Museum of Anthropology, Beloit College.* R. White and L. Breitborde (eds.). Beloit, Wisconsin: Bulletin of the Logan Museum of Anthropology, New Series, 1(2), 245-248.

FIELD, H., 1955, *The Track of Man*, London: Peter Davies.

HAUSER, O., 1911, *Le Périgord préhistorique,* Le Bugue, Réjou.

HAUSER, O., 1916, *La Micoque: Die Kultur Einer Neuen Diluvialrasse,* Leipzig: Verlag Von Veit.

KIDDER, H. AND L., 1932, Fouilles du Puy-de-Lacan (Corrèze), *Revue Archéologique,* 35: p. 1-33.

KIDDER, H. AND L., 1936, Le Puy de Lacan et ses gravures magdaleniennes, *L'Anthropologie,* 40: p. 17-31.

MACCURDY, G.G., 1914a, La Combe, a Paleolithic cave in the Dordogne, *American Anthropologist,* NS 16: p. 157-184.

MACCURDY, G.G., 1914b, Palaeolithic art as represented in the collections of the American Museum of Natural History. *The American Museum Journal.* 14: p. 225-237.

MACCURDY, G.G., 1931, The abri des Merveilles at castel-Merle near Sergeac (Dordogne), *Bulletin of the American School of Prehistoric Research,* 7: p. 12-23.

MATTHEWS, L., 1991, *Paleolithic assemblages from the Viré Collection, Logan Museum of Anthropology: Jouclas, Rivière-de-Tulle and Combe-Cullier.* Masters thesis, Department of Anthropology, New York University.

MATTHEWS, L., 1992, Paleolithic assemblages from the sites of Jouclas, Rivière de Tulle and Combe-Cullier from the Viré collection of the Logan Museum, *French Paleolithic Collections in the Logan Museum of Anthropology, Beloit College,* R. White and L. Breitborde (eds.), Beloit, Wisconsin: Bulletin of the Logan Museum of Anthropology, New Series, 1(2), p. 121-194.

NESBITT, P., 1928, *A Study of the Aurignacian Site La Ruth (France),* Masters thesis, University of Chicago.

PERRY, D., 1993, *The French Magdalenian sites of abri Mège and grotte de la Mairie (Périgord, France): an archaeological analysis of artifacts in the Field Museum of Natural History, Chicago..* Masters thesis, Department of Anthropology, New York University.

PEYRONY, D., 1926, *Rapport au Ministère d'Instruction Publique et Beaux-Arts.*

PEYRONY, D., 1946, Le gisement préhistorique de l'Abri Cellier, au Ruth, commune de Tursac (Dordogne), *Gallia,* 4: p. 294-301.

PEYRONY, E. AND DE SONNEVILLE-BORDES, D., 1959, L'Abri du Roc-Saint-Cirq, gisement magdalénien, commune de Saint-Cirq-du-Bugue (Dordogne), *Congrès Préhistorique de France,* p. 949-970.

POND, A.W., 1925, The oldest jewelry in the world, *Art and Archaeology,* 19 (3): p. 131-134.

ROMANOWICZ, J., 1991, *The Magdalenian Site of la Roche de Lalinde, Commune de Lalinde (Dordogne), France: The Artifacts in Historical and Archaeological Context.* Masters thesis, New York University.

SACKETT, J., 1968, Method and theory of Upper Paleolithic archeology in Southwestern France, *New Perspectives in Archeology.* S. and L. Binford (eds.), Chicago: Aldine, p. 61-83.

SIMEK, J., 1986, A Paleolithic sculpture from the Abri Labattut in the American Museum of Natural History collection, *Current Anthropology,* 27 (4): p. 402-407.

TOSELLO, G., 19987, *L'art mobilier sur support lithique en Périgord magdalénien: émergence, originalité et diffusion.* Thèse de Doctorat, Université de Paris 1 Panthéon-Sorbonne.

WHITE, R., 1980, *The Ami Collection of the National Museum of Canada: Geographic and Stratigraphic Context,* Report on file, National Museum of Canada, Contract No. 1630-9-002.

WHITE, R., 1986a, Rediscovering French Ice Age art, *Nature,* 320: p. 683-684.

WHITE, R., 1988, Objets magdaléniens provenant de l'Abri du Soucy (Dordogne): La collection de H.-M. Ami au Royal Ontario Museum, Toronto, Canada, *L'Anthropologie,* 92 (1): p. 29-40.

WHITE, R., 1992a, The history and research significance of the Logan Museum's French Paleolithic collections, *French Paleolithic Collections in the Logan Museum of Anthropology, Beloit College,* R. White and L. Breitborde (eds.), Beloit, Wisconsin: Bulletin of the Logan Museum of Anthropology, New Series, 1(2), p. 1-38.

WHITE, R., 1992b, Bone, antler and ivory objects from Abri Blanchard, commune de Sergeac (Dordogne), France, *French Paleolithic Collections in the Logan Museum of Anthropology, Beloit College,* R. White and L. Breitborde (eds.), Beloit, Wisconsin: Bulletin of the Logan Museum of Anthropology, New Series, 1(2), p. 97-120.

WHITE, R., 1992c, A spear-thrower fragment from Laugerie-Haute, commune des Eyzies (Dordogne), France. *French Paleolithic Collections in the Logan Museum of Anthropology, Beloit College.* R. White and L. Breitborde (eds.). Beloit, Wisconsin: Bulletin of the Logan Museum of Anthropology, New Series, 1(2), 259-276.

WHITE, R. AND DOBRES, M., 1992, Fifteen Azilian pebbles from Mas d'Azil (Ariège), France. *French Paleolithic Collections in the Logan Museum of Anthropology, Beloit College.* R. White and L. Breitborde (eds.). Beloit, Wisconsin: Bulletin of the Logan Museum of Anthropology, New Series, 1(2), 353-367.

WHITE, R. AND KNECHT, H., 1992, Abri Cellier (or la Ruth {sic}), commune de Tursac (Dordogne): Results of the 1927 Beloit College excavations, *French Paleolithic Collections in the*

Logan Museum of Anthropology, Beloit College, R. White and L. Breitborde (eds.), Beloit, Wisconsin: Bulletin of the Logan Museum of Anthropology, New Series, 1(2), p. 39-96.

WHITE, R. AND ROUSSOT, A., 1992a, Two Upper Paleolithic representations of uncertain provenience. *French Paleolithic Collections in the Logan Museum of Anthropology, Beloit College*. R. White and L. Breitborde (eds.). Beloit, Wisconsin: Bulletin of the Logan Museum of Anthropology, New Series, 1(2), 347-352.

WHITE, R. AND ROUSSOT, A., 1992b, An engraved bear from the Grotte des Eyzies, commune des Eyzies (Dordogne), France. *French Paleolithic Collections in the Logan Museum of Anthropology, Beloit College*. R. White and L. Breitborde (eds.). Beloit, Wisconsin: Bulletin of the Logan Museum of Anthropology, New Series, 1(2), 249-258.

WHITE, R. AND WELTÉ, A-C., 1992, Bruniquel (Tarn-et-Garonne) ou le Soucy (Dordogne): Les tribulations d'un cheval à travers l'Atlantique, *L'Anthropologie*.